# Ibn Taymiyya on ʿAlī & Shi'ism

Five Select Fatwās

*Sheikh al-Islām*

Aḥmed ibn ʿAbdilḤalīm

Ibn Taymiyya

Translations and Annotations by

Abdullah Al-Rabbat

# خَمْسُ فتَاوَى

## فِي مَرْتَبَةِ عَلِيّ بنِ أَبِي طَالِبٍ رضي الله عنه وَفِي التَّشَيُّعِ

لِشَيْخِ الإِسْلَامِ

تَقِيِّ الدِّينِ أَبِي العَبَّاسِ أَحْمَدَ بنِ تَيْمِيَّةَ الحَرَّانِي

رَحِمَهُ اللهُ تَعَالَى

ترجمها إلى الإنجليزية وعلّق عليها

عبد الله بن محمد فراس الرّبّاط

First Edition, 2023
ISBN: 979-8-218-29345-1
Published by Damask Publishers

# Table of Contents

# Translator's Preface

*In the name of Allah, the Compassionate and Beneficent*

Praise be to Allah alone. I seek refuge in Him and implore Him for aid and guidance. May Allah bless our Prophet Muhammad ﷺ, his family, his companions, and all who follow in his blessed footsteps.

This is a brief collection of legal verdicts (*fatwas*) on ʿAlī ibn Abī Ṭālib and Shi'ism issued by the eminent scholar, *Sheikh al-Islām* Ibn Taymiyyah (Allah bestow mercy upon him). His expositions in these *fatwās*, which are found in *Majmūʿ al-Fatāwā*, not only shed light on the topics they address, but also showcase his methodical analysis and skill in deconstructing misconceptions by examining their underlying premises. His approach in these *fatwas*, as well as his other works, provides an erudite framework with respect to these contentious subjects, in contrast to many of the ungrounded polemics that plague much of today's online discourse.

I previously published a translated epistle of Ibn Taymiyya, titled, "*Ibn Taymiyya's Cordial Letter of Advice to the Shia.*" This present work can be viewed as a subsequent installment of Taymiyyan literature on Shi'ism. It contains five *fatwas* issued by Ibn Taymiyya that address questions pertaining to Shi'ism, specifically ʿAlī ibn Abī Ṭālib's status and Rafidite heretics.

Broaching the topics of these *fatwas* is quite difficult without being misconstrued and attacked by zealous Shi'ites. Both mainstream Muslims and Shi'ites hold ʿAlī ibn Abī Ṭālib in high regard; however, mainstream Muslims maintain a sober and historically grounded perspective of his role and legacy. In contrast, a variety of Shi'ite factions and schools across history have held extremist views that exaggerate ʿAlī's role and status, crafting a caricature of ʿAlī that is decoupled from the "Historical ʿAlī." As a result, whenever mainstream Muslim scholars address such Shi'ite doctrines and mythologizations, they are often misinterpreted by Shi'ites as a denigration of ʿAlī himself, hence why Ibn Taymiyya is frequently maligned as a Nāsibī detractor of ʿAlī and *Ahlulbayt*, a slanderous accusation.

In several respects, it is akin to discussing Jesus' role and status from an Islamic perspective. While Muslims revere Jesus as one of the greatest prophets of God, they do not ascribe divinity to him. For Christians who see Jesus as divine, any description of Jesus that falls short of divinity is perceived as a sacrilegious offense. Likewise, Shi'ites who profess extremist views about ʿAlī will often perceive mainstream Muslims' reverence and praise of ʿAlī as a sacrilegious demotion of his rank and role within Islam, given that their praise is not aligned with the mythologized Shi'ite caricatures of his legacy.

This parallel drawn between extremist Shi'ites and Christians is not unprecedented, for it has been highlighted by several figures many centuries ago. The *tābiʿī*, al-Shaʿbī, said:

> ʿAlqama fought alongside ʿAlī at Ṣiffīn, and ʿAlqama said, "A group from this nation has perished due to its view on ʿAlī just as the Christians had perished by their view on ʿĪsā ibn Maryam (peace be upon him)."(1)

قال أبو بكر الخلال في «كتاب السنة»: أَخْبَرَنَا عَلِيٌّ، قَالَ: ثَنَا ابْنُ فُضَيْلٍ، عَنِ ابْنِ أَبِي خَالِدٍ، عَنْ عَامِرٍ، قَالَ: قَاتَلَ عَلْقَمَةُ مَعَ عَلِيٍّ حَتَّى عَرَجَ بِصِفِّينَ، فَقَالَ عَلْقَمَةُ: "لَقَدْ هَلَكَ قَوْمٌ مِنْ هَذِهِ الأُمَّةِ بِرَأْيِهِمْ فِي عَلِيٍّ كَمَا هَلَكَتِ النَّصَارَى فِي عِيسَى ابْنِ مَرْيَمَ عَلَيْهِ السَّلامُ".

It was also authentically recorded from the junior *tābiʿī*, Ibn Shihāb al-Zuhrī, that he said, "I have not seen a people more resemblant of the Christians than the Saba'ites," referring to the Rāfiḍā.(2)

---

(1) Kitāb al-Sunnah of Abū Bakr al-Khallāl (1/291)

(2) Kitāb al-Sharīʿa of al-ʾĀjurrī (5/2530)

قال الآجري في «كتاب الشريعة»: وَأَنْبَأَنَاهُ أَحْمَدُ بْنُ يَحْيَى الْحُلْوَانِيُّ، قَالَ: حَدَّثَنَا أَحْمَدُ بْنُ عَبْدِ اللَّهِ بْنِ يُونُسَ، عَنِ ابْنِ أَبِي ذِئْبٍ، عَنِ الزُّهْرِيِّ، قَالَ: " مَا رَأَيْتُ قَوْمًا أَشْبَهَ بِالنَّصَارَى مِنَ السَّبَائِيَّةِ." قَالَ أَحْمَدُ بْنُ يُونُسَ: هُمُ الرَّافِضَةُ.

In a weak prophetic tradition, the Messenger of Allah ﷺ is quoted telling ʿAlī, "In you is a parallel with Jesus: the Jews resented him to the extent that they slandered his own mother, while the Christians loved him to the extent that they ascribed to him a rank that is not his."(1)

قال عبد الله في زوائده على «المسند»: حَدَّثَنِي أَبُو مُحَمَّدٍ سُفْيَانُ بْنُ وَكِيعِ بْنِ الْجَرَّاحِ بْنِ مَلِيحٍ، حَدَّثَنَا خَالِدُ بْنُ مَخْلَدٍ، حَدَّثَنَا أَبُو غَيْلَانَ الشَّيْبَانِيُّ، عَنِ الْحَكَمِ بْنِ عَبْدِ الْمَلِكِ، عَنِ الْحَارِثِ بْنِ حَصِيرَةَ، عَنْ أَبِي صَادِقٍ، عَنْ رَبِيعَةَ بْنِ نَاجِدٍ، عَنْ عَلِيِّ بْنِ أَبِي طَالِبٍ رَضِيَ اللَّهُ عَنْهُ، قَالَ: دَعَانِي رَسُولُ اللَّهِ ﷺ فَقَالَ: " إِنَّ فِيكَ مِنْ عِيسَى مَثَلًا، أَبْغَضَتْهُ يَهُودُ حَتَّى بَهَتُوا أُمَّهُ، وَأَحَبَّتْهُ النَّصَارَى حَتَّى أَنْزَلُوهُ بِالْمَنْزِلِ الَّذِي لَيْسَ بِهِ "، أَلَا وَإِنَّهُ يَهْلِكُ فِيَّ اثْنَانِ: مُحِبٌّ يُقَرِّظُنِي بِمَا لَيْسَ فِيَّ، وَمُبْغِضٌ يَحْمِلُهُ شَنَآنِي عَلَى أَنْ يَبْهَتَنِي، أَلَا إِنِّي لَسْتُ بِنَبِيٍّ، وَلَا يُوحَى إِلَيَّ، وَلَكِنِّي أَعْمَلُ بِكِتَابِ اللَّهِ وَسُنَّةِ نَبِيِّهِ ﷺ مَا اسْتَطَعْتُ، فَمَا أَمَرْتُكُمْ مِنْ طَاعَةِ اللَّهِ، فَحَقٌّ عَلَيْكُمْ طَاعَتِي فِيمَا أَحْبَبْتُمْ وَكَرِهْتُمْ.

Within the *fatwas* published in this volume, Ibn Taymiyya's wording is carefully and precisely crafted such that its profundity, at some points, may be elusive to an untrained eye. In many of his arguments, it could be said that he simultaneously wears the hat of an analytical scientist and that of a meticulous artist. Not only is his acute attention to detail impressive in this regard, but also his ability to string together his observations in a certain fashion and order, ultimately giving rise to a vibrant and cohesive mosaic grounded in reason and the proof-texts of the *Shariah*.

(1) Musnad Aḥmed ibn Ḥanbal (2/469)

In other settings, one may also encounter an Ibn Taymiyya whose pen seems to be struggling to keep pace with his thoughts, resulting in more convoluted writings and works. In my translation and annotation of these *fatwas*, I tried enabling the readers to appreciate such instances to the best of my ability; alas, some things are only appreciated to their fullest extent by an acquainted scholarly eye.

In regards to Shi'ism, Ibn Taymiyya penned an encyclopedic refutation of it titled, *Minhāj al-Sunnah al-Nabawiyya Fī Naqḍ Kalām al-Shīʿa wa-l-Qadariyya.* It is a brilliant and comprehensive text that deconstructs a polemical book authored by the Twelver heretic, Ibn al-Muṭahhar al-Ḥillī (d. 726). It appears that several of the *fatwas* selected in this volume are closely related to Ibn Taymiyya's *Minhāj al-Sunnah,* as several portions therein seem to be summarized sections and arguments from *Minhāj al-Sunnah.*

Needless to say, the titles that precede each *fatwa* in this book are my summarizations, not titles penned by Ibn Taymiyya himself. The five *fatwās* in this book vary in their length, and the second and third *fatwas* constitute the core of this book. I have organized these *fatwās* in a specific order that should hopefully prove to be insightful and complimentary to their contents. All in all, I pray that this compilation benefits the readers and inspires further reading and enlightenment on their end.

# Fatwā #1
# On ʿAlī Being from *Ahlulbayt* and *Ṣalāt* Upon Him

## The Question

Ibn Taymiyya (Allah bestow mercy upon him) was asked about a man who claims that ʿAlī ibn Abī Ṭālib is not from *Ahlulbayt*; and that it is impermissible to invoke *ṣalāt* upon on him;[1] and that invoking *ṣalāt* upon him is an innovation (*bidʿa*). [2]

## The Answer

He responded:

Regarding ʿAlī being from *Ahlulbayt*, this is undisputed between the Muslims, and it is more obvious among the Muslims than to need evidence. In fact, he is the best of *Ahlulbayt* and the best of Banī Hāshim after the Prophet ﷺ.

---

(1) Invoking *ṣalāt* upon a person is to say, "*Ṣallā Allāh ʿAlayh*," or, "*Allāhummā Ṣallī ʿAlayh.*" It is a specific prayer that Allah honor a person in a specific manner. Some scholars stated that it is an invocation of Allah's mercy. See al-Rawḍ al-Murbiʿ of al-Buhūtī (p. 27).

(2) Majmūʿ al-Fatāwā (4/496). I commence this book with this *fatwā* of *Sheikh al-Islām* to highlight how his perception of ʿAlī is one of reverence and respect, contrary to what is regularly claimed by Shi'te extremists who dishonestly malign him as a Nāṣibī detractor of ʿAlī. It should contextualize the remainder of his *fatwās* mentioned in this book *in shāʾa Allah.*

# الفتوى الأولى

## في كون علي بن أبي طالب رضي الله عنه من أهل البيت، والصلاة عليه منفردا

### السؤال

سُئِلَ – رحمه الله – عَنْ رَجُلٍ قَالَ عَنْ عَلِيِّ بْنِ أَبِي طَالِبٍ رضي الله عنه إِنَّهُ لَيْسَ مِنْ أَهْلِ الْبَيْتِ وَلَا تَجُوزُ الصَّلَاةُ عَلَيْهِ، وَالصَّلَاةُ عَلَيْهِ بِدْعَةٌ.

### الجواب

فَأَجَابَ:

أَمَّا كَوْنُ عَلِيِّ بْنِ أَبِي طَالِبٍ مِنْ أَهْلِ الْبَيْتِ فَهَذَا مِمَّا لَا خِلَافَ فِيهِ بَيْنَ الْمُسْلِمِينَ، وَهُوَ أَظْهَرُ عِنْدَ الْمُسْلِمِينَ مِنْ أَنْ يَحْتَاجَ إِلَى دَلِيلٍ؛ بَلْ هُوَ أَفْضَلُ أَهْلِ الْبَيْتِ وَأَفْضَلُ بَنِي هَاشِمٍ بَعْدَ النَّبِيِّ ﷺ.

It has been established that the Prophet ﷺ engulfed ʿAlī, Fāṭima, Ḥasan, and Ḥusayn with his cloak and said, "O Allah, these are my household, so cleanse them of impurities and purify them thoroughly."(1)

As for *ṣalāt* upon ʿAlī alone, this will depend on the answer to the following question: is it permissible to single out anyone asides from the Prophet ﷺ in *ṣalāt*, such as the statement, "O Allah *ṣallī ʿalā* ʿUmar or ʿAlī"?

The scholars have disagreed in that regard. Mālik,(2) al-Shāfiʿī,(3) and a group of the Ḥanbalīs(4) have held that *ṣalāt* upon an individual in isolation is only to be done for the Prophet ﷺ, as has been reported from Ibn ʿAbbās that he said, "I know of no *ṣalāt* that should be invoked upon a person except the Prophet ﷺ."(5)

However, *Imām* Aḥmed and the majority of his companions held that there is nothing wrong in that because ʿAlī ibn Abī Ṭālib ؓ said to ʿUmar ibn al-Khaṭṭāb ؓ, "May Allah's *ṣalāt* be upon you (*Ṣallā Allāh ʿalayk*)."(6) This position is more correct and more worthy.

---

(1) Musnad Aḥmed ibn Ḥanbal (44/118-119, 44/173-174, 44/217). The variant of this ḥadīth cited by Ibn Taymiyya is that of Um Salama. It should be noted that there exist other variants of the ḥadīth reported from multiple *Ṣaḥāba*. See Ṣaḥīḥ Muslim (4/1883) and Musnad Aḥmed ibn Ḥanbal (28/195).

(2) Al-Shifā Bi-Taʿrīf Ḥuqūq al-Muṣṭafā of al-Qāḍī ʿIyāḍ (p. 577-578)

(3) Nihāyat al-Maṭlab Fī Dirāyat al-Madhab of al-Juwaynī (3/371-372), al-Majmūʿ Sharḥ al-Muhaḏḏab of al-Nawawī (6/171-172)

(4) Masāʾil al-Imām Aḥmed – Riwāyat Abī Dāwūd (p. 113), Majmūʿ al-Fatāwā of Ibn Taymiyya (22/473)

(5) Muṣannaf Ibn Abī Shayba (6/47). The isnād unto Ibn ʿAbbās is authentic.

(6) This is reported by Jaʿfar al-Ṣādiq, from his father, from Jābir ibn ʿAbdillāh through several sources, and it is an authentic statement of ʿAlī. See Tārīkh al-Madīna of Ibn Shabba (3/937-938, 3/940), and al-Mustadrak ʿAlā al-Ṣaḥīḥayn of al-Ḥākim (5/277).

وَقَدْ ثَبَتَ عَنْ النَّبِيِّ ﷺ أَنَّهُ أَدَارَ كِسَاءَهُ عَلَى عَلِيٍّ وَفَاطِمَةَ وَحَسَنٍ وَحُسَيْنٍ فَقَالَ: "اللَّهُمَّ هَؤُلَاءِ أَهْلُ بَيْتِي فَأَذْهِبْ عَنْهُمْ الرِّجْسَ وَطَهِّرْهُمْ تَطْهِيرًا."

وَأَمَّا الصَّلَاةُ عَلَيْهِ مُنْفَرِدًا فَهَذَا يَنْبَنِي عَلَى أَنَّهُ هَلْ يُصَلَّى عَلَى غَيْرِ النَّبِيِّ ﷺ مُنْفَرِدًا؟ مِثْلَ أَنْ يَقُولَ: اللَّهُمَّ صَلِّ عَلَى عُمَرَ أَوْ عَلِيٍّ؟

وَقَدْ تَنَازَعَ الْعُلَمَاءُ فِي ذَلِكَ. فَذَهَبَ مَالِكٌ وَالشَّافِعِيُّ وَطَائِفَةٌ مِنْ الْحَنَابِلَةِ: إلَى أَنَّهُ لَا يُصَلَّى عَلَى غَيْرِ النَّبِيِّ ﷺ مُنْفَرِدًا، كَمَا رُوِيَ عَنْ ابْنِ عَبَّاسٍ أَنَّهُ قَالَ: "لَا أَعْلَمُ الصَّلَاةَ تَنْبَغِي عَلَى أَحَدٍ إلَّا عَلَى النَّبِيِّ ﷺ."

وَذَهَبَ الْإِمَامُ أَحْمَد وَأَكْثَرُ أَصْحَابِهِ إلَى أَنَّهُ لَا بَأْسَ بِذَلِكَ، لِأَنَّ عَلِيَّ بْنَ أَبِي طَالِبٍ رَضِيَ اللَّهُ عَنْهُ قَالَ لِعُمَرِ بْنِ الْخَطَّابِ رَضِيَ اللَّهُ عَنْهُ: "صَلَّى اللَّهُ عَلَيْك." وَهَذَا الْقَوْلُ أَصَحُّ وَأَوْلَى.

Nonetheless, exclusively invoking *ṣalāt* for a specific individual from the *Ṣaḥāba* or kin, like ʿAlī or others, in a manner that mirrors the Prophet ﷺ, such that it becomes a recognized slogan involving that individual's name: that is the innovation (*bidʿa*).[1]

(1) This point was made by several scholars prior to Ibn Taymiyya, such as al-Juwaynī. Refer to footnote #3 on page 7.

وَلَكِنَّ إِفْرَادَ وَاحِدٍ مِنْ الصَّحَابَةِ وَالْقُرَابَةِ كَعَلِيٍّ أَوْ غَيْرِهِ بِالصَّلَاةِ عَلَيْهِ دُونَ غَيْرِهِ مُضَاهَاةً لِلنَّبِيِّ ﷺ - بِحَيْثُ يُجْعَلُ ذَلِكَ شِعَارًا مَعْرُوفًا بِاسْمِهِ - هَذَا هُوَ الْبِدْعَةُ.

# Fatwā #2
# On ʿAlī's Purported Supremacy

## The Question

*Sheikh al-Islām* (Allah bestow mercy upon him) was asked about a man who adheres to the Sunnah but has doubts regarding the superiority of the three [caliphs] over ʿAlī because of the Prophet's ﷺ statement to ʿAlī, "You are from me, and I am from you;" and his statement, "You are to me as Aaron was to Moses;" and his statement, "I shall give the banner to a man who loves Allah and His messenger...;" and his statement, "Whoever I am his *mawlā*, then ʿAlī is his *mawlā*. O Allah befriend whoever befriends him, and take an enemy whoever takes him as an enemy...;" and his statement, "I remind you of Allah regarding my household;" and Allah's statement, "Let us call our children and your children [Quran 3:61];" and Allah's statement, "Has there come upon man [Quran 76:1];" and Allah's statement, "Here are two adversaries feuding regarding their Lord. [Quran 22:19]"(1)

(1) Majmūʿ al-Fatāwā (4/414). Some of these references are abrupt excerpts from the Quran or Sunnah that are cited in the context of ʿAlī's merits. They will be elucidated and referenced later as Ibn Taymiyya addresses each tradition individually.

# الفتوى الثانية

## في الجواب على من فضَّلَ عليًّا على الشيْخيْن ﵄

### السؤال

سُئِلَ شَيْخُ الْإِسْلَامِ – رَحِمَهُ اللَّهُ تَعَالَى – عَنْ رَجُلٍ مُتَمَسِّكٍ بِالسُّنَّةِ وَيَحْصُلُ لَهُ رِيبَةٌ فِي تَفْضِيلِ الثَّلَاثَةِ عَلَى عَلِيٍّ لِقَوْلِهِ لَهُ: {أَنْتَ مِنِّي وَأَنَا مِنْك}، وَقَوْلِهِ: {أَنْتَ مِنِّي بِمَنْزِلَةِ هَارُونَ مِنْ مُوسَى}، وَقَوْلِهِ: {لَأُعْطِيَنَّ الرَّايَةَ رَجُلًا يُحِبُّ اللَّهَ وَرَسُولَهُ} . . إلَخْ، وَقَوْلِهِ: {مَنْ كُنْت مَوْلَاهُ فَعَلِيٌّ مَوْلَاهُ اللَّهُمَّ وَالِ مَنْ وَالَاهُ وَعَادِ مَنْ عَادَاهُ} . . إلَخْ، وَقَوْلِهِ: " {أُذَكِّرُكُمْ اللَّهَ فِي أَهْلِ بَيْتِي}، وَقَوْلِهِ سُبْحَانَهُ: {فَقُلْ تَعَالَوْا نَدْعُ أَبْنَاءَنَا وَأَبْنَاءَكُمْ} الْآيَةَ، وقَوْله تَعَالَى {هَلْ أَتَى عَلَى الْإِنْسَانِ} الْآيَةَ، وَقَوْلِهِ: {هَذَانِ خَصْمَانِ اخْتَصَمُوا فِي رَبِّهِمْ} الْآيَةَ.

## The Answer

He responded:

First, it should be understood that superiority is when the superior one possesses distinct merits (*khaṣāʾiṣ*) that the lesser one lacks. If they are both on equal footing, yet one possesses some distinct merits, then he is deemed superior. Shared merits, however, do not entail superiority of one over the other.

With this understanding, it is evident that Abū Bakr al-Ṣiddīq's distinctive merits were exclusive to him; however, 'Alī's merits where shared among others.[1]

The Prophet's statement, "If I were to choose a bosom friend from mankind, then I would have chosen Abū Bakr as a bosom friend;"[2] and his statement, "Seal every pass-through to the mosque except Abū Bakr's pass-through;"[3] and his statement, "Among the people to whom I am most indebted for his companionship and wealth is Abū Bakr."[4] These are three exclusive merits not shared with anyone else.

The first highlights the Prophet's unmatched indebtedness to Abū Bakr for his companionship and wealth. The second is his statement, "Seal every pass-through...," which is a specification of Abū Bakr over everyone else. Some of the liars sought to ascribe a similar merit to 'Alī; however, the authentic cannot be countered with the fabricated.[5]

---

(1) The point is that the merits of 'Alī referenced in the initial question were not unique to him per se. However, a host of Abū Bakr's renowned merits were exclusively embodied in Abū Bakr (Allah be pleased with them both).

(2) Ṣaḥīḥ al-Bukhārī (1/100-101, 5/4, 8/152), Ṣaḥīḥ Muslim (4/1854-1856)

(3) Ṣaḥīḥ al-Bukhārī (1/100-101, 5/4, 5/57-58), Ṣaḥīḥ Muslim (4/1854-1856)

(4) Refer to footnote #2.

(5) Some unreliable transmitters have reported that it was 'Alī whose door was exclusively left unblocked, and all routes to this tradition are demonstrably

## الجواب

فَأَجَابَ:

يَجِبُ أَنْ يُعْلَمَ أَوَّلًا أَنَّ التَّفْضِيلَ إِذَا ثَبَتَ لِلْفَاضِلِ مِنَ الْخَصَائِصِ مَا لَا يُوجَدُ مِثْلُهُ لِلْمَفْضُولِ. فَإِذَا اسْتَوَيَا وَانْفَرَدَ أَحَدُهُمَا بِخَصَائِصَ كَانَ أَفْضَلَ. وَأَمَّا الْأُمُورُ الْمُشْتَرَكَةُ فَلَا تُوجِبُ تَفْضِيلَهُ عَلَى غَيْرِهِ.

وَإِذَا كَانَ كَذَلِكَ فَفَضَائِلُ الصِّدِّيقِ رضي الله عنه الَّتِي تَمَيَّزَ بِهَا لَمْ يُشْرِكْهُ فِيهَا غَيْرُهُ، وَفَضَائِلُ عَلِيٍّ مُشْتَرَكَةٌ.

وَذَلِكَ أَنَّ قَوْلَهُ: {لَوْ كُنْت مُتَّخِذًا مِنْ أَهْلِ الْأَرْضِ خَلِيلًا لَاتَّخَذْت أَبَا بَكْرٍ خَلِيلًا}، وَقَوْلَهُ: {لَا يَبْقَى فِي الْمَسْجِدِ خَوْخَةٌ إِلَّا سُدَّتْ، إِلَّا خَوْخَةُ أَبِي بَكْرٍ}، وَقَوْلَهُ: {إِنَّ أَمَنَّ النَّاسِ عَلَيَّ فِي صُحْبَتِهِ وَذَاتِ يَدِهِ أَبُو بَكْرٍ}، وَهَذَا فِيهِ ثَلَاثُ خَصَائِصَ لَمْ يُشْرِكْهُ فِيهَا أَحَدٌ.

الْأُولَى: أَنَّهُ لَيْسَ لِأَحَدٍ مِنْهُمْ عَلَيْهِ فِي صُحْبَتِهِ وَمَالِهِ مِثْلُ مَا لِأَبِي بَكْرٍ. الثَّانِيَةُ: قَوْلُهُ: {لَا يَبْقَى فِي الْمَسْجِدِ} . . . إِلَخْ، وَهَذَا تَخْصِيصٌ لَهُ دُونَ سَائِرِهِمْ. وَأَرَادَ بَعْضُ الْكَذَّابِينَ أَنْ يَرْوِيَ لِعَلِيٍّ مِثْلَ ذَلِكَ، وَالصَّحِيحُ لَا يُعَارِضُهُ الْمَوْضُوعُ .

---

unreliable. Ibn al-Jawzī addressed those traditions in Kitāb al-Mawḍūʿāt (1/363-368).

The third is that his statement, "If I were to choose a bosom friend," is a proof-text (*naṣṣ*) indicating that no one else was worthy of that intimate level of friendship, if attainable, except Abū Bakr. Had there been anyone superior to him, then that individual would have been more worthy of it had it been attainable.

Similarly, the Prophet's ﷺ instruction of Abū Bakr to lead the people in prayer during his illness is among the distinct merits.(1) Likewise, the Prophet's ﷺ entrustment of Abū Bakr with oversight of the Ḥajj so that he may establish the Sunnah and obliterate the traces of the *Jāhiliyya* is among his distinct merits.(2) Similarly, his statement in the authentic ḥadīth, "Summon your father and brother so that I may write a document for Abū Bakr."(3) Such ḥadīths are abundant, and they demonstrate that there was none equivalent to him among the *Ṣaḥāba.*

Regarding the Prophet's ﷺ statement [to ʿAlī], "You are from me, and I am from you,"(4) he had also expressed this notion to other than ʿAlī. He expressed it to Salmān and to the Ashʿariyyīn.(5)

---

(1) Ṣaḥīḥ al-Bukhārī (1/133-134, 1/136-137), Ṣaḥīḥ Muslim (1/313-316)

(2) Ṣaḥīḥ al-Bukhārī (2/153), Ṣaḥīḥ Muslim (2/982), Ṣaḥīḥ Ibn Khuzayma (p. 674), Ṣaḥīḥ Ibn Ḥibbān (4/192), al-Sīra al-Nabawiyya of Ibn Hishām (2/461)

(3) ʿĀʾisha (Allah be pleased with her) reported that the Prophet said during his illness, "Summon for me your father and brother so that I may have something written down for Abū Bakr, as I fear that a wishful person may aspire to something, saying, 'I am more worthy.' However, Allah and the believers refuse anyone other than Abū Bakr." See Ṣaḥīḥ Muslim (4/1857) and Musnad Aḥmed ibn Ḥanbal (42/50).

(4) Ṣaḥīḥ al-Bukhārī (3/184-185, 5/141)

(5) It seems to be the case that "Salmān" here is a typographical error and that the intended word was "Julaybīb." See Minhāj al-Sunnah of Ibn Taymiyya (5/29-30, 7/392). The Prophet uttered such a statement with respect to Julaybīb, a companion of his who was martyred at an expedition. Upon finding his corpse surrounded by the corpses of seven disbelievers, the Prophet said, "He killed seven, and they then killed him. This one is from

الثَّالِثَةُ: قَوْلُهُ: {لَوْ كُنْت مُتَّخِذًا خَلِيلًا} نَصٌّ فِي أَنَّهُ لَا أَحَدَ مِنَ الْبَشَرِ اسْتَحَقَّ الْخُلَّةَ لَوْ أَمْكَنْت إِلَّا هُوَ، وَلَوْ كَانَ غَيْرُهُ أَفْضَلَ مِنْهُ لَكَانَ أَحَقَّ بِهَا لَوْ تَقَعُ.

وَكَذَلِكَ أَمْرُهُ لَهُ أَنْ يُصَلِّيَ بِالنَّاسِ مُدَّةَ مَرَضِهِ مِنَ الْخَصَائِصِ. وَكَذَلِكَ تَأْمِيرُهُ لَهُ فِي الْمَدِينَةِ عَلَى الْحَجِّ لِيُقِيمَ السُّنَّةَ وَيَمْحَقَ آثَارَ الْجَاهِلِيَّةِ، فَإِنَّهُ مِنْ خَصَائِصِهِ. وَكَذَلِكَ قَوْلُهُ فِي الْحَدِيثِ الصَّحِيحِ: {ادْعُ أَبَاكَ وَأَخَاكَ حَتَّى أَكْتُبَ لِأَبِي بَكْرٍ كِتَابًا}. وَأَمْثَالُ هَذِهِ الْأَحَادِيثِ كَثِيرَةٌ تُبَيِّنُ أَنَّهُ لَمْ يَكُنْ فِي الصَّحَابَةِ مَنْ يُسَاوِيهِ.

وَأَمَّا قَوْلُهُ: {أَنْتَ مِنِّي وَأَنَا مِنْك}، فَقَدْ قَالَهَا لِغَيْرِهِ، وَقَالَهَا لِسَلْمَانَ[1] وَالأَشْعَرِيِّينَ.

---

me, and I am from him! This one is from me, and I am from him!" See Ṣaḥīḥ Muslim (4/1918-1919).

As for the instance where the Prophet uttered this statement with respect to the Ashʿarī tribe, he said, "[...] They are from me, and I am from them." See Ṣaḥīḥ al-Bukhārī (3/138), Ṣaḥīḥ Muslim (4/1944-1945).

(1) لعل الأصل: "لـجُلَيْبِيب." وبه احتج الشيخ في مواضع من «منهاج السنة»، وهو أليق، والله تعالى أعلم.

Allah's statement in the Quran, "They swear by Allah that they are from you, but they are not [Quran 9:56]," and the Prophet's ﷺ statement, "Whoever cheats us is not one of us,"(1) entail that one who refrains from these major sins is "from us." Consequently, every believer with thorough faith is from the Prophet, and the Prophet is from him.

His statement to [ʿAlī] regarding Ḥamza's daughter, "You are from me, and I am from you," and his statement to Zayd, "You are our brother and *mawlā*,"(2) is not confined to Zayd. It encompasses all of his *mawlās* as well.

In a similar vein is his statement, "I shall hand the banner...," which is the most authentic ḥadīth transmitted on ʿAlī's merits.(3) Some liars have added to the report that Abū Bakr and ʿUmar had initially taken the banner and subsequently fled. Yet, in the *Ṣaḥīḥ*, it is reported that ʿUmar said, "That was the only day in which I desired leadership."(4)

This ḥadīth is a refutation of the Nāṣibīs who disparage ʿAlī, but it is not an exclusive merit of ʿAlī. Rather, any Muslim of thorough faith loves Allah and His Messenger and is beloved to Allah and His Messenger ﷺ. Allah said, "[O you who believe! Whoever of you apostatizes from his religion], then Allah shall bring a people whom He loves and who love Him. [Quran 5:54]" Those people are those who combated the apostates, and their leader was Abū Bakr.

---

(1) Ṣaḥīḥ Muslim (1/99)

(2) Ṣaḥīḥ al-Bukhārī (3/184-185, 5/141-142)

(3) When at Khaybar, the Prophet said, "I shall hand the banner to a man who loves Allah and His Messenger, and Allah shall facilitate the victory through him." The Prophet then handed the banner to ʿAlī, and the conquest later ensued. See Ṣaḥīḥ al-Bukhārī (4/53) and Ṣaḥīḥ Muslim (4/1871-1872).

(4) Ṣaḥīḥ Muslim (4/1871-1872). The implication here is that ʿUmar was not given the banner earlier and that the accretions about ʿUmar being given the banner and subsequently fleeing from battle are inaccurate. See Minhāj al-Sunnah of Ibn Taymiyya (7/366).

وَقَالَ تَعَالَى: {وَيَحْلِفُونَ بِاللَّهِ إِنَّهُمْ لَمِنْكُمْ وَمَا هُمْ مِنْكُمْ}، وَقَوْلُهُ ﷺ: {مَنْ غَشَّنَا فَلَيْسَ مِنَّا وَمَنْ حَمَلَ عَلَيْنَا السِّلَاحَ فَلَيْسَ مِنَّا}، يَقْتَضِي أَنَّ مَنْ يَتْرُكُ هَذِهِ الْكَبَائِرَ يَكُونُ مِنَّا. فَكُلُّ مُؤْمِنٍ كَامِلُ الْإِيمَانِ فَهُوَ مِنَ النَّبِيِّ ﷺ وَالنَّبِيُّ مِنْهُ.

وَقَوْلُهُ فِي ابْنَةِ حَمْزَةَ: {أَنْتَ مِنِّي وَأَنَا مِنْكَ}، وَقَوْلُهُ لِزَيْدٍ: ( {أَنْتَ أَخُونَا وَمَوْلَانَا}، لَا يَخْتَصُّ بِزَيْدٍ بَلْ كُلُّ مَوَالِيهِ كَذَلِكَ.

وَكَذَلِكَ قَوْلُهُ: {لَأُعْطِيَنَّ الرَّايَةَ} . . إِلَخْ، هُوَ أَصَحُّ حَدِيثٍ يُرْوَى فِي فَضْلِهِ. وَزَادَ فِيهِ بَعْضُ الْكَذَّابِينَ أَنَّهُ أَخَذَهَا أَبُو بَكْرٍ وَعُمَرُ فَهَرَبَا. وَفِي الصَّحِيحِ أَنَّ عُمَرَ قَالَ: "مَا أَحْبَبْتُ الْإِمَارَةَ إِلَّا يَوْمَئِذٍ."

فَهَذَا الْحَدِيثُ رَدٌّ عَلَى النَّاصِبَةِ الْوَاقِعِينَ فِي عَلِيٍّ، وَلَيْسَ هَذَا مِنْ خَصَائِصِهِ. بَلْ كُلُّ مُؤْمِنٍ كَامِلُ الْإِيمَانِ يُحِبُّ اللَّهَ وَرَسُولَهُ وَيُحِبُّهُ اللَّهُ وَرَسُولُهُ ﷺ. قَالَ تَعَالَى: {فَسَوْفَ يَأْتِي اللَّهُ بِقَوْمٍ يُحِبُّهُمْ وَيُحِبُّونَهُ}، وَهُمُ الَّذِينَ قَاتَلُوا أَهْلَ الرِّدَّةِ وَإِمَامُهُمْ أَبُو بَكْرٍ.

In the *Ṣaḥīḥ*, it is reported that the Prophet ﷺ was asked, "Who among the people is most beloved to you?" He replied, "ʿĀ'isha." The questioner then asked, "And among the men?" The Prophet replied, "Her father."(1) This is among Abū Bakr's exclusive merits.

As for the Prophet's ﷺ statement, "Are you not content that you are to me as Aaron was to Moses?" he uttered it during the expedition of Tabūk when he left ʿAlī behind in-charge of Medīna. It was thus said, "He left him behind because he disdained him." Traditionally, whenever the Prophet ﷺ departed on an expedition, he would leave behind a man from his *Ummah* in-charge, and there would be able men from the believers in Medīna. At Tabūk, however, he let no one stay behind, so none stayed behind except those with valid excuses or sinners. This particular appointment in his absence consequently was less prestigious, leading some of the hypocrites to disparage ʿAlī. The Prophet thus reassured ʿAlī, "I did not leave you behind because of a deficiency in you, for Moses had left Aaron behind, and he was his partner in the message. Are you not content with that?"(2)

It is known that the Prophet ﷺ had previously left behind others in-charge, and they too held this rank in relation to the Prophet ﷺ. This was not one of ʿAlī's distinct merits. Had this appointment of ʿAlī in the Prophet's absence surpassed other appointments, its implications would not have eluded ʿAlī, who subsequently pursued the Prophet ﷺ in tears.

---

(1) Ṣaḥīḥ al-Bukhārī (5/5, 5/166), Ṣaḥīḥ Muslim (4/1856)

(2) This is Ibn Taymiyya's exposition of what the Prophet's statement implied, an it is not a literal quote. See Ṣaḥīḥ al-Bukhārī (5/19, 6/3) and Ṣaḥīḥ Muslim (5/1870-1871).

وَفِي الصَّحِيحِ {أَنَّهُ سَأَلَهُ: أَيُّ النَّاسِ أَحَبُّ إِلَيْك؟ قَالَ: عَائِشَةُ. قَالَ: فَمِنْ الرِّجَالِ؟ قَالَ: أَبُوهَا}، وَهَذَا مِنْ خَصَائِصِهِ.

وَأَمَّا قَوْلُهُ: {أَمَا تَرْضَى أَنْ تَكُونَ مِنِّي بِمَنْزِلَةِ هَارُونَ مِنْ مُوسَى}، قَالَهُ فِي غَزْوَةِ تَبُوكَ لَمَّا اسْتَخْلَفَهُ عَلَى الْمَدِينَةِ. فَقِيلَ: اسْتَخْلَفَهُ لِبُغْضِهِ إِيَّاهُ، وَكَانَ النَّبِيُّ ﷺ إِذَا غَزَا اسْتَخْلَفَ رَجُلًا مِنْ أُمَّتِهِ وَكَانَ بِالْمَدِينَةِ رِجَالٌ مِنْ الْمُؤْمِنِينَ الْقَادِرِينَ، وَفِي غَزْوَةِ تَبُوكَ لَمْ يَأْذَنْ لِأَحَدِ فَلَمْ يَتَخَلَّفْ أَحَدٌ إِلَّا لِعُذْرِ أَوْ عَاصٍ. فَكَانَ ذَلِكَ الِاسْتِخْلَافُ ضَعِيفًا، فَطَعَنَ بِهِ الْمُنَافِقُونَ بِهَذَا السَّبَبِ. فَبَيَّنَ لَهُ أَنِّي لَمْ أَسْتَخْلِفْك لِنَقْصِ عِنْدِي، فَإِنَّ مُوسَى اسْتَخْلَفَ هَارُونَ وَهُوَ شَرِيكُهُ فِي الرِّسَالَةِ، أَفَمَا تَرْضَى بِذَلِكَ؟

وَمَعْلُومٌ أَنَّهُ اسْتَخْلَفَ غَيْرَهُ قَبْلَهُ، وَكَانُوا مِنْهُ بِهَذِهِ الْمَنْزِلَةِ؛ فَلَمْ يَكُنْ هَذَا مِنْ خَصَائِصِهِ. وَلَوْ كَانَ هَذَا الِاسْتِخْلَافُ أَفْضَلَ مِنْ غَيْرِهِ لَمْ يَخَفْ عَلَى عَلِيٍّ وَلَحِقَهُ يَبْكِي.

What demonstrates this is that after the aforementioned event, the Prophet ﷺ placed Abū Bakr in-charge of ʿAlī in year 9. The Prophet's subsequent dispatch of ʿAlī to annul the pacts is not one of ʿAlī's unique merits. It was the norm that a person's pact could only be annulled or ratified by a man from his own household. Anyone from the Prophet's ﷺ household could have fulfilled that task; however, ʿAlī was the foremost among Banī Hāshim after the Messenger of Allah ﷺ, making him more suited than the others to proceed.

With the Prophet's ﷺ appointment of Abū Bakr in-charge after his statement [to ʿAlī], "Are you not content...," we recognized that the tradition does not entail ʿAlī's analogousness to Aaron in all respects. Instead, the Prophet simply highlighted a parallel between ʿAlī and Aaron in terms of deputization, and it is not among his distinct merits.

The Prophet had also drawn a parallel between Abū Bakr and Jesus and Abraham, and between ʿUmar and Noah and Moses (Peace and blessings be upon them). That occurred when they both provided counsel concerning the captives [at Badr].(1) These analogies are superior to the ʿAlī-Aaron analogy, and they do not entail an equivalency in rank with those messengers. Drawing an analogy between two things due to their similarity in some respects is replete in the Quran, Sunnah, and the Arabic language.

As for his statement, "Whoever I am his *mawlā*, then ʿAlī is his *mawlā*. O Allah, befriend whoever befriends him, and take as an enemy whoever takes him as an enemy," this is not reported in the canonical collections except al-Tirmiḏī.(2) There, the tradition only says, "Whoever I am his *mawlā*, then ʿAlī is his *mawlā*."

---

(1) Muṣannaf Ibn Abī Shayba (20/320-321), Musnad Aḥmed ibn Ḥanbal (6/138-140)

(2) Al-Jāmiʿ al-Kabīr of al-Tirmiḏī (6/79). Ibn Māja also reported it in his *Sunan*; see Sunan Ibn Māja (1/88).

وَمِمَّا بَيَّنَ ذَلِكَ أَنَّهُ بَعْدَ هَذَا أَمَّرَ عَلَيْهِ أَبَا بَكْرٍ سَنَةَ تِسْعٍ. وَكَوْنُهُ بَعَثَهُ لِنَبْذِ الْعُهُودِ لَيْسَ مِنْ خَصَائِصِهِ؛ لِأَنَّ الْعَادَةَ لَمَّا جَرَتْ أَنَّهُ لَا يَنْبِذُ الْعُهُودَ وَلَا يَعْقِدُهَا إِلَّا رَجُلٌ مِنْ أَهْلِ بَيْتِهِ، فَأَيُّ شَخْصٍ مِنْ عِتْرَتِهِ نَبَذَهَا حَصَلَ الْمَقْصُودُ. وَلَكِنَّهُ أَفْضَلُ بَنِي هَاشِمٍ بَعْدَ رَسُولِ اللَّهِ ﷺ، فَكَانَ أَحَقَّ النَّاسِ بِالتَّقَدُّمِ مِنْ سَائِرِهِمْ.

فَلَمَّا أَمَّرَ أَبَا بَكْرٍ بَعْدَ قَوْلِهِ: {أَمَا تَرْضَى} . . . إلَخْ، عَلِمْنَا أَنَّهُ لَا دَلَالَةَ فِيهِ عَلَى أَنَّهُ بِمَنْزِلَةِ هَارُونَ مِنْ كُلِّ وَجْهٍ، وَإِنَّمَا شَبَّهَهُ بِهِ فِي الِاسْتِخْلَافِ خَاصَّةً، وَذَلِكَ لَيْسَ مِنْ خَصَائِصِهِ.

وَقَدْ شَبَّهَ النَّبِيُّ ﷺ أَبَا بَكْرٍ بِإِبْرَاهِيمَ وَعِيسَى وَشَبَّهَ عُمَرَ بِنُوحٍ وَمُوسَى عَلَيْهِمْ الصَّلَاةُ وَالسَّلَامُ لَمَّا أَشَارَا فِي الْأَسْرَى. وَهَذَا أَعْظَمُ مِنْ تَشْبِيهِ عَلِيٍّ بِهَارُونَ، وَلَمْ يُوجِبْ ذَلِكَ أَنْ يَكُونَا بِمَنْزِلَةِ أُولَئِكَ الرُّسُلِ. وَتَشْبِيهُ الشَّيْءِ بِالشَّيْءِ لِمُشَابَهَتِهِ فِي بَعْضِ الْوُجُوهِ كَثِيرٌ فِي الْكِتَابِ وَالسُّنَّةِ وَكَلَامِ الْعَرَبِ.

وَأَمَّا قَوْلُهُ: {مَنْ كُنْت مَوْلَاهُ فَعَلِيٌّ مَوْلَاهُ، اللَّهُمَّ وَالِ مَنْ وَالَاهُ} . . . إلَخْ، فَهَذَا لَيْسَ فِي شَيْءٍ مِنْ الْأُمَّهَاتِ إلَّا فِي التِّرْمِذِيِّ، وَلَيْسَ فِيهِ إلَّا: {مَنْ كُنْت مَوْلَاهُ فَعَلِيٌّ مَوْلَاهُ}.

Regarding the additional clause, it is not in the ḥadīth.(1) *Imām* Aḥmed was asked about it, to which he said, "It is a Kufan addition.(2)" It certainly is dubious for several reasons, one of them being that the Truth does not revolve around a single individual besides the Prophet ﷺ.(3)

---

(1) Referring to the clause, "O Allah, befriend whoever befriends him, and take as an enemy whoever takes him as an enemy," which is not present in al-Tirmiḏī's report.

(2) In fact, *Imām* Aḥmed reported a tradition in his *Musnad* which alludes to this. He reported therein from Abū Maryam and another companion of ʿAlī, from ʿAlī that the Prophet said on the Day of Ghadīr Khum, "Whoever I am his *mawlā*, then ʿAlī is his *mawlā*." The tradition then concludes with a comment from one of the transmitters, saying, "The people later added [to the tradition], "O Allah, befriend whoever befriends him, and take as an enemy whoever takes him as an enemy." See Musnad Aḥmed ibn Ḥanbal (2/434).

Sharīk al-Qāḍī, prior to *Imām* Aḥmed, noted that the forgers of Kufa later introduced this accretion into the ḥadīth. See al-Kāmil Fī Ḍuʿafāʾ al-Rijāl (3/425). The Mutazilite scholar, al-Jāḥiẓ, similarly stated that this accretion was exclusively introduced to the tradition through some Shi'ite transmitters. See al-ʿUthmāniyya (p. 144). In *Minhāj al-Sunnah*, Ibn Taymiyya mentioned that this accretion was dubious per consensus of the scholars of ḥadīth. See Minhāj al-Sunnah of Ibn Taymiyya (7/55).

An example of how this accretion was dubiously introduced into some variants of tradition can be observed in Zayd ibn Arqam's report. At the end of one ḥadīth from Zayd ibn Arqam that does not include this accretion, ʿAṭiyya al-Awfī asked Zayd, "Did you hear the Prophet say, 'O Allah, befriend whoever befriends him, and take as an enemy whoever takes him as an enemy'?" Zayd ibn Arqam said, "I only inform you of what I had heard." See Musnad Aḥmed ibn Ḥanbal (32/29). Nonetheless, in spite of Zayd's negation of this accretion, some unreliable transmitters later ascribed it to Zayd himself! See Musnad Aḥmed ibn Ḥanbal (32/73-74, 38/218-219).

(3) Here, Ibn Taymiyya singles out one of the reasons, which is its *matn's* dubious nature, and he discusses one particularity pertinent to this dubious *matn*. The other reasons alluded to by Ibn Taymiyya include the unreliability of isnāds behind this clause and its absence in the more reliable variants of this account, amidst a host of other noteworthy observations and indicators.

وَأَمَّا الزِّيَادَةُ فَلَيْسَتْ فِي الْحَدِيثِ. وَسُئِلَ عَنْهَا الْإِمَامُ أَحْمَد فَقَالَ: "زِيَادَةٌ كُوفِيَّةٌ." وَلَا رَيْبَ أَنَّهَا كَذِبٌ لِوُجُوهٍ: أَحَدُهَا: أَنَّ الْحَقَّ لَا يَدُورُ مَعَ مُعَيَّنٍ إِلَّا النَّبِيَّ ﷺ.

Otherwise, it would have been obligatory to follow ʿAlī in everything he had uttered. It is known that the *Ṣaḥāba* and followers of ʿAlī disputed several matters with him where the proof-texts were in favor of those who disagreed with ʿAlī.(1) An example is the issue of a woman whose husband dies whilst she is pregnant.(2)

---

(1) Do note that Ibn Taymiyya wrote this *fatwā* in response to a question from someone who presumably was a righteous and reasonable person, and this point by Ibn Taymiyya thus would have been a valid retort: most reasonable Muslims would acknowledge that no one besides the Prophet should be emulated in an absolute sense.

Contemporary Shi'ites, however, would nod in glee at Ibn Taymiyya's argument, as their *modus operandi* is that ʿAlī ibn Abī Ṭālib was an infallible person who should be absolutely followed and emulated in everything he said and did. Nonetheless, Ibn Taymiyya's next statement embodies a response to that as well, for there are instances where ʿAlī's *ijtihad* proved to be contrary to more reliable proof-texts. Furthermore, the earlier arguments made by Ibn Taymiyya in this *fatwa* are implicit refutations of ʿAlī's purported infallibility. There is a lot more that may be argued and expounded in this context, though it does not take much to convince a sober and reasonable non-Shi'ite that ʿAlī (Allah be pleased with him) was an imperfect human like the remainder of the righteous companions and scholars.

(2) Regarding a woman whose husband died while she's pregnant, ʿAlī's position was that her waiting period (*ʿidda*) prior to her remarriage should be the longer of the two periods. The two periods being referenced are: (1) four months and ten days, or (2) the period of time remaining for her pregnancy. Thus, according to ʿAlī, if a pregnant woman's husband dies when she is in the ninth month of pregnancy, she should remain in her waiting period (*ʿidda*) for four months and ten days, as that is longer than the period of time remaining for her pregnancy. However, if a pregnant woman's husband dies while she is in the first month of her pregnancy, then her waiting period (*ʿidda*) would be her entire pregnancy, as that would be a longer period than the other option of four months and ten days.

This *fatwā* of ʿAlī conflicts with several authentic prophetic traditions and the fatwas of several prominent companions of the Prophet. The four schools, have all agreed that the waiting period of a pregnant widow before she can remarry ends immediately as soon as she gives birth, even if she were to give birth one hour after her husband's death, contrary to ʿAlī's *fatwa* (Allah be pleased with him). See Saḥīḥ al-Bukhārī (5/80, 6/155-156,

لِأَنَّهُ لَوْ كَانَ كَذَلِكَ لَوَجَبَ اتِّبَاعُهُ فِي كُلِّ مَا قَالَ. وَمَعْلُومٌ أَنَّ عَلِيًّا يُنَازِعُهُ الصَّحَابَةُ وَأَتْبَاعُهُ فِي مَسَائِلَ وُجِدَ فِيهَا النَّصُّ يُوَافِقُ مَنْ نَازَعَهُ، كَالْمُتَوَفَّى عَنْهَا زَوْجُهَا وَهِيَ حَامِلٌ.

---

7/56-57), Ṣaḥīḥ Muslim (2/1122). This position of the four schools, the majority of the Ṣaḥāba, and that of the authentic prophetic traditions is also more in-line with the apparent meaning of the Quran; see Quran 65:4.

Regarding his statement [in the report], "O Allah, grant victory to whomever aids him...," it is contrary to reality. Some people fought alongside ʿAlī on the Day of Ṣiffīn, yet they did not emerge victorious. Conversely, there were others who abstained from fighting, yet they were not forsaken. For instance, Saʿd [ibn Abī Waqqāṣ], who had conquered Iraq, did not fight alongside ʿAlī. In the same vein, Muʿāwiya's partisans and the Umayyads who had fought ʿAlī conquered many of the disbelievers' lands and were granted victory by Allah.

Similarly, his statement, "O Allah, befriend whoever befriends him, and take as an enemy whoever takes him as an enemy," is contrary to the core of Islam. The Quran has established that the believers remain brethren, even when engaged in combat and transgression against each other.(1)

As for his statement, "Whoever I am his *mawlā*, then ʿAlī is his *mawlā*," some scholars of ḥadīth, such as al-Bukhārī and others, criticized it.(2) Some declared it *ḥasan.* If indeed uttered by the Prophet ﷺ, then he did not intend it as a *wilāya* that was exclusive to ʿAlī. Rather, it signifies the communal affinity (*wilāya*), which is the affinity of faith that is shared among believers. The opposite of affinity (*al-muwālāt*) is animosity (*al-muʿādāt*), and the affinity of Muslims towards fellow Muslims over non-Muslims is obligatory without a doubt. Therefore, the ḥadīth embodies a refutation of the Nāṣibīs.

---

(1) This is a reference to Quran 49:9-10, where Allah said, "If two groups of believers fight each other, reconcile between them. But if one group aggresses against the other, fight the aggressing group until it complies with Allah's command. Once it has complied, reconcile between them with justice, and be equitable. Allah loves the equitable. The believers are brothers, so reconcile between your brothers."

(2) Ibn Taymiyya reported that Ibrāhīm al-Ḥarbī also criticized the tradition. See Minhāj al-Sunnah (7/319-320). Ibn Ḥazm also weakened the tradition. See al-Faṣl Fī al-Milal wa-l-Ahwāʾ wa-l-Niḥal (4/224).

وَقَوْلُهُ: {اللَّهُمَّ انْصُرْ مَنْ نَصَرَهُ} . . إلَخْ خِلَافُ الْوَاقِعِ. قَاتَلَ مَعَهُ أَقْوَامٌ يَوْمَ صِفِّين فَمَا انْتَصَرُوا، وَأَقْوَامٌ لَمْ يُقَاتِلُوا فَمَا خُذِلُوا؛ كَسَعْدِ الَّذِي فَتَحَ الْعِرَاقَ، لَمْ يُقَاتِلْ مَعَهُ. وَكَذَلِكَ أَصْحَابُ مُعَاوِيَةَ وَبَنِيَّ أُمَيَّةَ الَّذِينَ قَاتَلُوهُ، فَتَحُوا كَثِيرًا مِنْ بِلَادِ الْكُفَّارِ وَنَصَرَهُمْ اللَّهُ.

وَكَذَلِكَ قَوْلُهُ: {اللَّهُمَّ وَالِ مَنْ وَالَاهُ وَعَادِ مَنْ عَادَاهُ} مُخَالِفٌ لِأَصْلِ الْإِسْلَامِ، فَإِنَّ الْقُرْآنَ قَدْ بَيَّنَ أَنَّ الْمُؤْمِنِينَ إخْوَةٌ مَعَ قِتَالِهِمْ وَبَغْيِ بَعْضِهِمْ عَلَى بَعْضٍ.

وَقَوْلُهُ: {مَنْ كُنْت مَوْلَاهُ فَعَلِيٌّ مَوْلَاهُ} فَمِنْ أَهْلِ الْحَدِيثِ مَنْ طَعَنَ فِيهِ كَالْبُخَارِيِّ وَغَيْرِهِ، وَمِنْهُمْ مَنْ حَسَّنَهُ. فَإِنْ كَانَ قَالَهُ فَلَمْ يُرِدْ بِهِ وِلَايَةً مُخْتَصًّا بِهَا، بَلْ وِلَايَةً مُشْتَرَكَةً وَهِيَ وِلَايَةُ الْإِيمَانِ الَّتِي لِلْمُؤْمِنِينَ. وَالْمُوَالَاةُ ضِدُّ الْمُعَادَاةِ، وَلَا رَيْبَ أَنَّهُ يَجِبُ مُوَالَاةُ الْمُؤْمِنِينَ عَلَى سِوَاهُمْ، فَفِيهِ رَدٌّ عَلَى النَّوَاصِبِ.

Concerning the ḥadīth about ʿAlī donating his ring during prayer, it is falsehood by consensus of the experts. That is demonstrated through several means expounded elsewhere.(1)

As for his statement on the Day of Ghadīr Khum, "I remind of you of Allah regarding my household," it is not an exclusive merit [of ʿAlī]. He stands on equal footing with the rest of *Ahlulbayt* in this regard. The people most distant from the application of this ordinance are the Rāfiḍa, for they harbor hostility towards al-ʿAbbās, his descendants, and, indeed, towards the majority of *Ahlulbayt*, aligning with the disbelievers against them.(2)

Regarding the verse on *mubāhala*, it is not an exclusive merit [of ʿAlī].(3) In that event, the Prophet ﷺ summoned ʿAlī, Fāṭima, and their two sons, not because they were the foremost of the *Ummah*, but because they were his closest kin. As stated in the ḥadīth of the cloak, "O Allah, these are my household, so cleanse them of impurity and purify them thoroughly."(4) He thus prayed for them and specified them.

---

(1) Ibn Kathīr stated this tradition is inauthentic and that all of its routes are unreliable. See al-Bidāya wa-l-Nihāya (11/93-94). Ibn Taymiyya also addresses this tradition in detail in Minhāj al-Sunnah (7/10-31).

(2) Twelver sources embody disparagement of many Hashemites, descendents of al-Ḥasan, descendents of al-ʿAbbās and others who, for various reasons, did not conform to Twelver doctrines. As an example, see al-Kāfī of al-Kulaynī (1/142), Baṣā'ir al-Darājāt of al-Ṣaffār (p. 215).

(3) The verse in question is Quran 3:61, where Allah said, "And if anyone disputes with you about him, after the knowledge that has come to you, say, 'Come, let us call our children and your children, and our women and your women, and ourselves and yourselves, and let us invoke Allah's curse on the liars'."

Shi'ite polemicists argue that, "our children," refers to al-Ḥasan and al-Ḥusayn, and "our women," refers to Fāṭima. They thus argue that, "ourselves," in the verse is an instance where ʿAlī was equated with the Prophet's self, a supposedly great merit of ʿAlī. Ibn Taymiyya in this section refutes Shi'ite appeal to this verse and associated ḥadīths.

(4) Ṣaḥīḥ Muslim (4/1883), Musnad Aḥmed (28/195)

وَحَدِيثُ {التَّصَدُّقِ بِالْخَاتَمِ فِي الصَّلَاةِ} كَذِبٌ بِاتِّفَاقِ أَهْلِ الْمَعْرِفَةِ، وَذَلِكَ مُبَيَّنٌ بِوُجُوهٍ كَثِيرَةٍ مَبْسُوطَةٍ فِي غَيْرِ هَذَا الْمَوْضِعِ.

وَأَمَّا قَوْلُهُ يَوْمَ غَدِيرِ خُمٍّ: {أُذَكِّرُكُمُ اللَّهَ فِي أَهْلِ بَيْتِي} فَلَيْسَ مِنَ الْخَصَائِصِ، بَلْ هُوَ مُسَاوٍ لِجَمِيعِ أَهْلِ الْبَيْتِ. وَأَبْعَدُ النَّاسِ عَنْ هَذِهِ الْوَصِيَّةِ الرَّافِضَةُ، فَإِنَّهُمْ يُعَادُونَ الْعَبَّاسَ وَذُرِّيَّتَهُ، بَلْ يُعَادُونَ جُمْهُورَ أَهْلِ الْبَيْتِ وَيُعِينُونَ الْكُفَّارَ عَلَيْهِمْ.

وَأَمَّا آيَةُ الْمُبَاهَلَةِ فَلَيْسَتْ مِنْ الْخَصَائِصِ. بَلْ دَعَا عَلِيًّا وَفَاطِمَةَ وَابْنَيْهِمَا، وَلَمْ يَكُنْ ذَلِكَ لِأَنَّهُمْ أَفْضَلُ الْأُمَّةِ بَلْ لِأَنَّهُمْ أَخَصُّ أَهْلِ بَيْتِهِ، كَمَا فِي حَدِيثِ الْكِسَاءِ: {اللَّهُمَّ هَؤُلَاءِ أَهْلُ بَيْتِي فَأَذْهِبْ عَنْهُمْ الرِّجْسَ وَطَهِّرْهُمْ تَطْهِيرًا}. فَدَعَا لَهُمْ وَخَصَّهُمْ.

The term, *"al-anfus* (selves)," is used to signify a single category, as in Allah's statement, "Shall the believing men and women not think well of themselves? [Quran 24:12]" And when Allah said, "And kill yourselves [Quran 2:54]," meaning that you should kill each other.(1)

The Prophet's ﷺ statement [to ʿAlī], "You are from me, and I am from you," does not imply that ʿAlī shares his very essence. ʿAlī unquestionably is of paramount status among the Prophet's kin, and he more profoundly embodies the distinction of kinship and faith than the rest of the kin. This warranted his inclusion in the *mubāhala.* Nevertheless, this distinction does not preclude others unrelated to the Prophet ﷺ from surpassing ʿAlī. That is because the *mubāhala* was centered on relatives.

Concerning Allah's statement, "Here are two adversaries [Quran 22:19]," it is shared between ʿAlī, Ḥamza, and ʿUbayda.(2) In fact, it encompasses the rest of the Badrīs who share it with them as well.

---

(1) This verse is a reference to Quran 2:54, where Allah said, "And recall that Moses said to his people, 'O my people, you have done wrong to yourselves by worshiping the calf. So repent to your Maker, and kill yourselves. That would be better for you with your Maker.' So He turned to you in repentance. He is the Accepter of Repentance, the Merciful."

Ibn Taymiyya's argument here is that the Shi'ite interpretation of the word, "ourselves," in this context is a misunderstanding and misuse of the word's usage in Arabic. "Ourselves" in Arabic refers to a unified category of people. So when the verse says, "Let us call ourselves and yourselves," it means something like, "Let us call our people and your people." The verse does not entail an equivalence of ʿAlī and the Prophet or that they are of the same essence, as is claimed by Shi'ites.

(2) This is a reference to an authentic tradition where Abū Ḏarr stated that the verse, 'Here are two adversaries feuding regarding their Lord [Quran 22:19],' was revealed about the six men who dueled each other at the beginning of the Battle of Badr: ʿAlī, Ḥamza, ʿUbayda ibn al-Ḥārith, Shayba ibn Rabīʿa, ʿUtba ibn Rabīʿa, and al-Walīd ibn ʿUtba." See Ṣaḥīḥ al-Bukhārī (5/75, 6/98) and Ṣaḥīḥ Muslim (4/2323). It should not be misconstrued as a unique merit of ʿAlī (Allah be pleased with him).

وَالْأَنْفُس يُعَبَّرُ عَنْهَا بِالنَّوْعِ الْوَاحِدِ، كَقَوْلِهِ: {ظَنَّ الْمُؤْمِنُونَ وَالْمُؤْمِنَاتُ بِأَنْفُسِهِمْ خَيْرًا}، وَقَالَ: {فَاقْتُلُوا أَنْفُسَكُمْ} – أَيْ: يَقْتُلُ بَعْضُكُمْ بَعْضًا.

وَقَوْلُهُ: {أَنْتَ مِنِّي وَأَنَا مِنك} لَيْسَ الْمُرَادُ أَنَّهُ مِنْ ذَاتِهِ، وَلَا رَيْبَ أَنَّهُ أَعْظَمُ النَّاسِ قَدْرًا مِنْ الْأَقَارِبِ. فَلَهُ مِنْ مَزِيَّةِ الْقَرَابَةِ وَالْإِيمَانِ مَا لَا يُوجَدُ لِبَقِيَّةِ الْقَرَابَةِ، فَدَخَلَ فِي ذَلِكَ الْمُبَاهَلَةِ. وَذَلِكَ لَا يَمْنَعُ أَنْ يَكُونَ فِي غَيْرِ الْأَقَارِبِ مَنْ هُوَ أَفْضَلُ مِنْهُ، لِأَنَّ الْمُبَاهَلَةَ وَقَعَتْ فِي الْأَقَارِبِ.

وَقَوْلُهُ: {هَذَانِ خَصْمَانِ} الْآيَةَ فَهِيَ مُشْتَرَكَةٌ بَيْنَ عَلِيٍّ وَحَمْزَةَ وَعُبَيْدَةَ بَلْ وَسَائِرُ الْبَدْرِيِّينَ يُشَارِكُونَهُمْ فِيهَا.

Regarding *Sūrat al-Insān*, any claim that it was revealed specifically about ʿAlī, Fāṭima, and her two sons is a lie. That is because it is a Meccan *sūra*, while al-Ḥasan and al-Ḥusayn were born in Medīna.(1) Even if the claim's veracity were taken for granted, the chapter does not state that one who feeds the needy or an orphan is the foremost of the *Ṣaḥāba*. Rather, the verse is broad, encompassing anyone who commits to such acts.(2) It entails such a person's worthiness of reward for this deed, though other deeds, such as faith in Allah, prayer on time, and *jihād*, are superior.

---

(1) There is a debate about when this chapter was revealed, with some scholars stating it is a Meccan chapter and others stating it is a Medinite chapter. Nonetheless, Ibn Taymiyya's argument is a strong argument if the chapter proves to be a Meccan chapter. It should also be noted that his argument here is, more or less, a tangential argument that is based on a prior implicit observation, which is that there are no authentic traditions stating that this chapter was revealed about ʿAlī and/or his household.

(2) This is referring to Quran 76:8-11, where Allah said, "And they feed, for the love of Allah, the poor, the orphan, and the captive. 'We only feed you for the sake of Allah. We want from you neither compensation, nor gratitude. We dread from our Lord a frowning grim Day.' So Allah will protect them from the ills of that Day, and will grant them radiance and joy...."

وَأَمَّا سُورَةُ: {هَلْ أَتَى عَلَى الْإِنْسَانِ}، فَمَنْ قَالَ إِنَّهَا نَزَلَتْ فِيهِ وَفِي فَاطِمَةَ وَابْنَيْهِمَا فَهَذَا كَذِبٌ لِأَنَّهَا مَكِّيَّةٌ. وَالْحَسَنُ وَالْحُسَيْنُ إِنَّمَا وُلِدَا فِي الْمَدِينَةِ. وَبِتَقْدِيرِ صِحَّتِهِ فَلَيْسَ فِيهِ أَنَّهُ مَنْ أَطْعَمَ مِسْكِينًا وَيَتِيمًا وَأَسِيرًا أَفْضَلُ الصَّحَابَةِ. بَلْ الْآيَةُ عَامَّةٌ مُشْتَرَكَةٌ فِيمَنْ فَعَلَ هَذَا وَتَدُلُّ عَلَى اسْتِحْقَاقِهِ لِلثَّوَابِ عَلَى هَذَا الْعَمَلِ، مَعَ أَنَّ غَيْرَهُ مِنْ الْأَعْمَالِ مِنْ الْإِيمَانِ بِاَللَّهِ وَالصَّلَاةِ فِي وَقْتِهَا وَالْجِهَادُ أَفْضَلُ مِنْهُ.

# Fatwā #3
# On ʿAlī's Purported Supremacy in Knowledge

## The Question

Ibn Taymiyya (Allah bestow mercy upon him) was asked about a disagreement between two men. One of them asserted, "Abū Bakr al-Ṣiddīq and ʿUmar ibn al-Khaṭṭāb (Allah be pleased with them) were more learned and knowledgeable than ʿAlī ibn Abī Ṭālib (Allah be pleased with him). The other said, "Rather, ʿAlī ibn Abī Ṭālib was more learned and knowledgeable than both Abū Bakr and ʿUmar."

Which of these two positions is more valid? Are these two ḥadīths, namely the Prophet's statements, "The most judicious of you is ʿAlī," and "I am the city of knowledge, and ʿAlī is its gate," authentic? If they are authentic, do they embody evidence that ʿAlī is more learned and knowledgeable than Abū Bakr and ʿUmar (Allah be pleased with them all)?

Furthermore, if someone claims the existence of a consensus among the Muslims that ʿAlī (Allah be pleased with him) is more learned and knowledgeable than Abū Bakr and ʿUmar (Allah be pleased with them all), would he be correct or mistaken?[1]

---

(1) Majmūʿ al-Fatāwā (4/398)

# الفتوى الثالثة

## الجواب على من فضّل عليًّا على الشيخين من جهة علمه رضي الله عنهم

### السؤال

وَسُئِلَ – رَحِمَهُ اللَّهُ – عَنْ رَجُلَيْنِ اخْتَلَفَا فَقَالَ أَحَدُهُمَا: "أَبُو بَكْرٍ الصِّدِّيقُ وَعُمَرُ بْنُ الْخَطَّابِ رضي الله عنهما أَعْلَمُ وَأَفْقَهُ مِنْ عَلِيِّ بْنِ أَبِي طَالِبٍ رضي الله عنه." وَقَالَ الْآخَرُ: "بَلْ عَلِيُّ بْنُ أَبِي طَالِبٍ رضي الله عنه أَعْلَمُ وَأَفْقَهُ مِنْ أَبِي بَكْرٍ وَعُمَرَ رضي الله عنهما."

فَأَيُّ الْقَوْلَيْنِ أَصْوَبُ؟ وَهَلْ هَذَانِ الْحَدِيثَانِ، وَهُمَا قَوْلُهُ ﷺ: {أَقْضَاكُمْ عَلِيٌّ}، وَقَوْلُهُ: {أَنَا مَدِينَةُ الْعِلْمِ وَعَلِيٌّ بَابُهَا} صَحِيحَانِ؟ وَإِذَا كَانَا صَحِيحَيْنِ فَهَلْ فِيهِمَا دَلِيلٌ أَنَّ عَلِيًّا أَعْلَمُ وَأَفْقَهُ مِنْ أَبِي بَكْرٍ وَعُمَرَ – رضي الله عنهم أَجْمَعِينَ؟

وَإِذَا ادَّعَى مُدَّعٍ أَنَّ إِجْمَاعَ الْمُسْلِمِينَ عَلَى أَنَّ عَلِيًّا رضي الله عنه أَعْلَمُ وَأَفْقَهُ مِنْ أَبِي بَكْرٍ وَعُمَرَ - رضي الله عنهم أَجْمَعِينَ – يَكُونُ مُحِقًّا أَوْ مُخْطِئًا؟

## The Answer

He responded:

All praise belongs to Allah. None of the regarded scholars of the Muslims have held that ʿAlī is more knowledgeable and learned than both Abū Bakr and ʿUmar, not even more than Abū Bakr alone.(1) One who claims a consensus in that regard is among the most ignorant and deceitful of people.

In fact, several scholars have cited the scholars' consensus that Abū Bakr was superior in knowledge to ʿAlī. Among them is *Imām* Manṣūr ibn ʿAbdilJabbār al-Samʿānī al-Marwazī, an *Imām* of the Sunnah from the followers of al-Shāfiʿī. He mentioned in his book, *Taqwīm al-Adillā ʿAlā al-Imām*, the consensus of the scholars of the Sunnah that Abū Bakr was more knowledgeable than ʿAlī.

I am unaware of any of the renowned *Imāms* disputing that. How could it be disputed when Abū Bakr used to issue *fatwā*, order, forbid, adjudicate, and deliver sermons in the Prophet's presence?

---

(1) There is a tradition from the Meccan jurist, ʿAṭā' ibn Abī Rabāḥ, which presents him being asked, "Were there among Muḥammad's companions anyone more knowledgeable than ʿAlī?" He responded, "No, by Allah I know not of anyone" See Muṣannaf Ibn Abī Shayba (17/123). It appears that there is missing context from the tradition, as ʿAṭā' elsewhere reported traditions on this in more qualified, non-absolute terms. See Kitāb al-Ṭabaqāt al-Kabīr of Ibn Saʿd (2/293). Similar qualified and non-absolute statements were reported from ʿAṭā''s teacher, Ibn ʿAbbās. See Muṣannaf Ibn Abū Sayba (15/510) and Kitāb al-Ṭabaqāt al-Kabīr of Ibn Saʿd (2/293).

Ibn Taymiyya briefly touches on this point later in this *fatwa*, and his aforementioned point should generally be perceived as valid. There are a variety of explicit and subtle evidences demonstrating Abū Bakr's superiority to ʿAlī in knowledge (Allah be pleased with them both), as shall be elucidated in this *fatwa*.

## الجواب

فَأَجَابَ:

الْحَمْدُ لِلَّهِ، لَمْ يَقُلْ أَحَدٌ مِنْ عُلَمَاءِ الْمُسْلِمِينَ الْمُعْتَبَرِينَ: إِنَّ عَلِيًّا أَعْلَمُ وَأَفْقَهُ مِنْ أَبِي بَكْرٍ وَعُمَرَ، بَلْ وَلَا مِنْ أَبِي بَكْرٍ وَحْدَهُ. وَمُدَّعِي الْإِجْمَاعِ عَلَى ذَلِكَ مِنْ أَجْهَلِ النَّاسِ وَأَكْذَبِهِمْ.

بَلْ ذَكَرَ غَيْرُ وَاحِدٍ مِنَ الْعُلَمَاءِ إِجْمَاعَ الْعُلَمَاءِ عَلَى أَنَّ أَبَا بَكْرٍ الصِّدِّيقَ أَعْلَمُ مِنْ عَلِيٍّ. مِنْهُمُ الْإِمَامُ مَنْصُورُ بْنُ عَبْدِ الْجَبَّارِ السَّمْعَانِي المروذي [المروزي]؛ أَحَدُ أَئِمَّةِ السُّنَّةِ مِنْ أَصْحَابِ الشَّافِعِيِّ. ذَكَرَ فِي كِتَابِهِ «تَقْوِيمُ الْأَدِلَّةِ عَلَى الْإِمَامِ» إِجْمَاعَ عُلَمَاءِ السُّنَّةِ عَلَى أَنَّ أَبَا بَكْرٍ أَعْلَمُ مِنْ عَلِيٍّ.

وَمَا عَلِمْت أَحَدًا مِنَ الْأَئِمَّةِ الْمَشْهُورِينَ يُنَازِعُ فِي ذَلِكَ. وَكَيْفَ وَأَبُو بَكْرٍ الصِّدِّيقُ كَانَ بِحَضْرَةِ النَّبِيِّ ﷺ يُفْتِي وَيَأْمُرُ وَيُنْهِي وَيَقْضِي وَيَخْطُبُ؟

[This is] as he used to do when he and the Prophet ﷺ would embark to call people to Islam,[1] during their mutual migration,[2] on the day of Ḥunayn,[3] and during other expeditions of the Prophet.[4] Throughout these instances, the Prophet ﷺ would remain silent in affirmation and agreement to Abū Bakr's words. This rank was unique to Abū Bakr.

When the Prophet ﷺ sought counsel from the people of knowledge, understanding, and insight from his companions, he used to place Abū Bakr and ʿUmar at the forefront in counsel. When in the company of the Messenger, both would precede the other companions in speech and knowledge, as was the case with the Prophet's ﷺ deliberation regarding the captives of Badr. On that occasion and others, Abū Bakr and ʿUmar were the foremost to speak.[5]

It has been reported in ḥadīth that the Prophet ﷺ said to them both, "If you both concur on a matter, I would not oppose you."[6] Consequently, their shared positions are a valid evidence (*ḥujja*) according to one of two positions held by the scholars, and it is one of the two positions reported from Aḥmed ibn Ḥanbal. This is in contrast to the positions of ʿUthmān and ʿAlī.[7]

---

(1) Ṣaḥīḥ al-Bukhārī (5/9-10, 5/46, 6/127), al-Mustadrak ʿAlā al-Ṣaḥīḥayn (5/266)

(2) Ṣaḥīḥ al-Bukhārī (4/201-202, 3/69), Ṣaḥīḥ Muslim (4/2309-2310)

(3) Ṣaḥīḥ al-Bukhārī (4/92, 5/155, 9/69), Ṣaḥīḥ Muslim (3/1370-1371)

(4) Ṣaḥīḥ al-Bukhārī (3/193-194), Muṣannaf ʿAbdirrazzāq (5/321-330). There are tens of other sources that can be cited in this context.

(5) Muṣannaf Ibn Abī Shayba (20/321), Musnad Aḥmed ibn Ḥanbal (6/138-139), Ṣaḥīḥ Muslim (3/1403-1404)

(6) Musnad Aḥmed ibn Ḥanbal (29/517-518). The isnād for this report embodies weakness, as it is a tradition of Shahr ibn Ḥawshab. The other isnāds to this tradition are all weak as well. Nonetheless, given a host of other texts, it appears to be reflective of a reality at the time.

(7) See al-ʿUdda Fī Uṣūl al-Fiqh of al-Qāḍī Abū Yaʿlā (4/1198-1204), Iʿlām al-Muwaqqiʿīn of Ibn al-Qayyim (5/546-547, 5/553)

كَمَا كَانَ يَفْعَلُ ذَلِكَ إِذَا خَرَجَ هُوَ وَأَبُو بَكْرٍ يَدْعُو النَّاسَ إِلَى الْإِسْلَامِ وَلَمَّا هَاجَرَا جَمِيعًا وَيَوْمَ حنين وَغَيْرِ ذَلِكَ مِنَ الْمَشَاهِدِ، وَالنَّبِيُّ ﷺ سَاكِتٌ يُقِرُّهُ عَلَى ذَلِكَ وَيَرْضَى بِمَا يَقُولُ، وَلَمْ تَكُنْ هَذِهِ الْمَرْتَبَةُ لِغَيْرِهِ.

وَكَانَ النَّبِيُّ ﷺ فِي مُشَاوَرَتِهِ لِأَهْلِ الْعِلْمِ وَالْفِقْهِ وَالرَّأْيِ مِنْ أَصْحَابِهِ يُقَدِّمُ فِي الشُّورَى أَبَا بَكْرٍ وَعُمَرَ. فَهُمَا اللَّذَانِ يَتَقَدَّمَانِ فِي الْكَلَامِ وَالْعِلْمِ بِحَضْرَةِ الرَّسُولِ عليه السلام عَلَى سَائِرِ أَصْحَابِهِ، مِثْلُ قِصَّةِ مُشَاوَرَتِهِ فِي أَسْرَى بَدْرٍ، فَأَوَّلُ مَنْ تَكَلَّمَ فِي ذَلِكَ أَبُو بَكْرٍ وَعُمَرُ؛ وَكَذَلِكَ غَيْرُ ذَلِكَ.

وَقَدْ رُوِيَ فِي الْحَدِيثِ أَنَّهُ قَالَ لَهُمَا: {إِذَا اتَّفَقْتُمَا عَلَى أَمْرٍ لَمْ أُخَالِفْكُمَا}. وَلِهَذَا كَانَ قَوْلُهُمَا حُجَّةً فِي أَحَدِ قَوْلَيْ الْعُلَمَاءِ، وَهُوَ إِحْدَى الرِّوَايَتَيْنِ عَنْ أَحْمَدَ. وَهَذَا بِخِلَافِ قَوْلِ عُثْمَانَ وَعَلِيٍّ.

In the *Sunan*, it is reported from the Prophet ﷺ that he said, "Follow the two who succeed me: Abū Bakr and ʿUmar."(1) He did not bestow this to anyone other than them. In fact, it is confirmed that he said, "Adhere to my Sunnah and the Sunnah of the rightly guided caliphs after me. Cling to it with your molars. Beware of innovated matters, for every innovation (*bidʿa*) is a misguidance."(2)

He thus commanded adherence to the Sunnah of the rightly-guided caliphs, spanning the four *Imāms*. However, he singled out Abū Bakr and ʿUmar in emulation. The rank of an individual who is emulated in both his actions and his precedents set for the Muslims is superior to the rank of one who is merely emulated in his precedents.

In *Ṣaḥīḥ Muslim*, it is reported that the Prophet's ﷺ companions were once traveling with him, to which he remarked, "If the people obey Abū Bakr and ʿUmar, they will be guided."(3)

---

(1) Al-Mustadrak ʿAlā al-Ṣaḥīḥayn (5/245-247). Al-Ḥākim authenticated this tradition; however, it contains a subtle defect. See Kitāb ʿIlāl al-Ḥadīth of Ibn Abī Ḥātim (6/444-446). The other routes for this tradition embody weakness, and Allah knows best.

(2) Al-Jāmiʿ al-Kabīr of al-Tirmiḏī (4/408-409), Ṣaḥīḥ Ibn Ḥibbān (4/114), al-Mustadrak of al-Ḥākim (1/390-391). Al-Tirmiḏī, Ibn Ḥibbān, al-Ḥākim, and others authenticated the tradition.
Imām Aḥmed ibn Ḥanbal cited this tradition as proof that Abū Bakr, ʿUmar, ʿUthmān and ʿAlī's precedents constitute a Sunnah. See Masā'il al-Imām Aḥmed – Riwāyat Abī Dāwūd (p. 369).

(3) Ṣaḥīḥ Muslim (1/472-473)

وَفِي السُّنَنِ عَنْهُ أَنَّهُ قَالَ: {اقْتَدُوا بِاللَّذَيْنِ مِنْ بَعْدِي: أَبِي بَكْرٍ وَعُمَرَ}، وَلَمْ يَجْعَلْ هَذَا لِغَيْرِهِمَا. بَلْ ثَبَتَ عَنْهُ أَنَّهُ قَالَ: {عَلَيْكُمْ بِسُنَّتِي وَسُنَّةِ الْخُلَفَاءِ الرَّاشِدِينَ الْمَهْدِيِّينَ مِنْ بَعْدِي. تَمَسَّكُوا بِهَا وَعَضُّوا عَلَيْهَا بِالنَّوَاجِذِ، وَإِيَّاكُمْ وَمُحْدَثَاتِ الْأُمُورِ، فَإِنَّ كُلَّ بِدْعَةٍ ضَلَالَةٌ}.

فَأَمَرَ بِاتِّبَاعِ سُنَّةِ الْخُلَفَاءِ الرَّاشِدِينَ. وَهَذَا يَتَنَاوَلُ الْأَئِمَّةَ الْأَرْبَعَةَ. وَخَصَّ أَبَا بَكْرٍ وَعُمَرَ بِالِاقْتِدَاءِ بِهِمَا. وَمَرْتَبَةُ الْمُقْتَدَى بِهِ فِي أَفْعَالِهِ وَفِيمَا سَنَّهُ لِلْمُسْلِمِينَ فَوْقَ سُنَّةِ الْمُتَّبِعِ فِيمَا سَنَّهُ فَقَطْ.

وَفِي صَحِيحِ مُسْلِمٍ أَنَّ أَصْحَابَ النَّبِيِّ ﷺ كَانُوا مَعَهُ فِي سَفَرٍ فَقَالَ: {إِنْ يُطِعْ الْقَوْمُ أَبَا بَكْرٍ وَعُمَرَ يَرْشُدُوا}.

It has also been established that Ibn ʿAbbās, when issuing legal verdicts (*fatwas*), would first consult with the Book of Allah. If he did not find anything therein, then he would refer to the precedents established by the Messenger of Allah ﷺ. If he did not find anything therein, he would refer to the opinions of Abū Bakr and ʿUmar.(1) He typically did not deal with ʿUthmān and ʿAlī in the same manner. Ibn ʿAbbās was the sage of the *Ummah* and the most knowledgeable and learned of the *Ṣaḥāba* of his time. He used to issue *fatwa* based on Abū Bakr and ʿUmar's opinions, prioritizing them over other companions' opinions. It has been established that the Prophet ﷺ said [about Ibn ʿAbbās], "O Allah, grant him understanding of the faith and knowledge interpretation."(2)

Furthermore, Abū Bakr and ʿUmar's had a distinct proximity to the Prophet ﷺ which surpassed that of others, with Abū Bakr's proximity to the Prophet ﷺ being even more profound. Abū Bakr used to stay up with him for most of the night, discussing matters of knowledge, the faith, and the Muslims' public interests.

As reported by Abū Bakr ibn Abī Shayba, he said: Abū Muʿāwiya informed us, from al-Aʿmash, from Ibrāhīm, from ʿAlqama, from ʿUmar, he said, "The Messenger of Allah ﷺ used to converse into the night at Abū Bakr's, discussing the Muslims' affairs with Abū Bakr whilst I was with him."(3)

---

(1) Muṣannaf Ibn Abī Shayba (11/608), Al-Mustadrak ʿAlā al-Ṣaḥīḥayn (1/449). Al-Ḥākim commented on the tradition saying, "It is authentic according to the standard of al-Bukhārī and Muslim..."

(2) Musnad Aḥmed ibn Ḥanbal (4/225, 4/244), Ṣaḥīḥ Ibn Ḥibbān (4/261). The core of the tradition is reported in the *Ṣaḥīḥayn* without the clause, "and knowledge in interpretation" See Ṣaḥīḥ al-Bukhārī (1/41) and Ṣaḥīḥ Muslim (4/1927).

(3) Muṣannaf Ibn Abī Shayba (4/459-461), Ṣaḥīḥ Ibn Khuzayma (p. 311). Another example among many is when the Prophet and Abū Bakr planned to migrate from Mecca to Medina together; see Ṣaḥīḥ al-Bukhārī (3/69).

وَقَدْ ثَبَتَ عَنْ ابْنِ عَبَّاسٍ أَنَّهُ كَانَ يُفْتِي مِنْ كِتَابِ اللَّهِ، فَإِنْ لَمْ يَجِدْ فَبِمَا سَنَّهُ رَسُولُ اللَّهِ ﷺ، فَإِنْ لَمْ يَجِدْ أَفْتَى بِقَوْلِ أَبِي بَكْرٍ وَعُمَرَ. وَلَمْ يَكُنْ يَفْعَلُ ذَلِكَ بِعُثْمَانَ وَعَلِيٍّ. وَابْنُ عَبَّاسٍ حَبْرُ الْأُمَّةِ وَأَعْلَمُ الصَّحَابَةِ وَأَفْقَهُهُمْ فِي زَمَانِهِ، وَهُوَ يُفْتِي بِقَوْلِ أَبِي بَكْرٍ وَعُمَرَ مُقَدِّمًا لِقَوْلِهِمَا عَلَى قَوْلِ غَيْرِهِمَا مِنَ الصَّحَابَةِ. وَقَدْ ثَبَتَ عَنْ النَّبِيِّ ﷺ أَنَّهُ قَالَ: {اللَّهُمَّ فَقِّهْهُ فِي الدِّينِ وَعَلِّمْهُ التَّأْوِيلَ}.

وَأَيْضًا فَأَبُو بَكْرٍ وَعُمَرُ كَانَ اخْتِصَاصُهُمَا بِالنَّبِيِّ ﷺ فَوْقَ اخْتِصَاصِ غَيْرِهِمَا. وَأَبُو بَكْرٍ كَانَ أَكْثَرَ اخْتِصَاصًا، فَإِنَّهُ كَانَ يَسْمُرُ عِنْدَهُ عَامَّةَ اللَّيْلِ يُحَدِّثُهُ فِي الْعِلْمِ وَالدِّينِ وَمَصَالِحِ الْمُسْلِمِينَ.

كَمَا رَوَى أَبُو بَكْرِ بْنُ أَبِي شَيْبَةَ: حَدَّثَنَا أَبُو مُعَاوِيَةَ، عَنْ الْأَعْمَشِ، عَنْ إبْرَاهِيمَ، عَنْ عَلْقَمَةَ، عَنْ عُمَرَ، قَالَ: {كَانَ رَسُولُ اللَّهِ ﷺ يَسْمُرُ عِنْدَ أَبِي بَكْرٍ فِي الْأَمْرِ مِنْ أُمُورِ الْمُسْلِمِينَ وَأَنَا مَعَهُ}.

In the *Ṣaḥīḥayn*, it is reported from ʿAbdurraḥmān ibn ʿAwf that the residents of *al-Ṣuffa* were impoverished people, and the Prophet ﷺ used to say, "Whoever possesses food sufficient for two people should invite a third person. Whoever possesses food sufficient for four should invite a fifth or sixth person." Abū Bakr thus returned with three people, and the Prophet ﷺ departed with ten. Abū Bakr then dined with the Prophet ﷺ, remaining with him until ʿIshā' prayer was prayed. He then rejoined the Prophet ﷺ and remained with him until the Messenger of Allah ﷺ became sleepy. Abū Bakr then returned to his house well into the night, and his wife then said to him, "What has barred you from tending to your guests?!" Abū Bakr, surprised, replied, "Have you not fed them dinner yet?!" She said, "They refused to eat until you returned. Dinner was offered to them, but they overwhelmingly refused to eat." And he mentioned the rest of the ḥadīth.(1) In one variant, it is said, "He used to converse with the Prophet ﷺ into the night."(2)

In the Prophet's ﷺ travel during the *Hijra*, he was accompanied by none other than Abū Bakr. On the day of Badr, none remained alongside the Prophet ﷺ in the canopy except Abū Bakr.(3) The Prophet ﷺ also said, "Among the people to whom we are most indebted for his companionship and wealth is Abū Bakr. If I were to choose a bosom friend from mankind, then I would have chosen Abū Bakr as a bosom friend."(4) This among the most authentic well-attested traditions in the authentic collections reported through many routes.(5)

---

(1) Ṣaḥīḥ al-Bukhārī (1/124), Ṣaḥīḥ Muslim (3/1627-1628)

(2) Perhaps he referring to the variant in Ṣaḥīḥ Muslim.

(3) Ṣaḥīḥ Muslim (3/1383-1385), Muṣannaf Ibn Abī Shayba (20/319), al-Sīra al-Nabawiyya of Ibn Hishām (1/553-554), Maghāzī al-Wāqidī (p. 74)

(4) Ṣaḥīḥ al-Bukhārī (1/100, 5/4, 8/152), Ṣaḥīḥ Muslim (4/1855)

(5) Elsewhere, Ibn Taymiyya mentioned that this tradition was mass-transmitted

وَفِي الصَّحِيحَيْنِ عَنْ عَبْدِ الرَّحْمَنِ بْنِ أَبِي بَكْرٍ: أَنَّ أَصْحَابَ الصُّفَّةِ كَانُوا نَاسًا فُقَرَاءَ؛ وَأَنَّ النَّبِيَّ ﷺ قَالَ: مَنْ كَانَ عِنْدَهُ طَعَامُ اثْنَيْنِ فَلْيَذْهَبْ بِثَالِثٍ، وَمَنْ كَانَ عِنْدَهُ طَعَامُ أَرْبَعَةٍ فَلْيَذْهَبْ بِخَامِسٍ أَوْ بِسَادِسٍ. وَأَنَّ أَبَا بَكْرٍ جَاءَ بِثَلَاثَةٍ وَانْطَلَقَ نَبِيُّ اللَّهِ ﷺ بِعَشَرَةٍ. وَأَنَّ أَبَا بَكْرٍ تَعَشَّى عِنْدَ النَّبِيِّ ﷺ وَسَلَّمَ ثُمَّ لَبِثَ حَتَّى صَلَّيْت الْعِشَاءَ ثُمَّ رَجَعَ، فَلَبِثَ حَتَّى نَعَسَ رَسُولُ اللَّهِ ﷺ. فَجَاءَ بَعْدَ مَا مَضَى مِنْ اللَّيْلِ مَا شَاءَ اللَّهُ، قَالَتْ امْرَأَتُهُ: "مَا حَبَسَك عَنْ أَضْيَافِك؟" قَالَ: "أَوْ مَا عَشَّيْتِهِمْ؟!" قَالَتْ: "أَبَوْا حَتَّى تَجِيءَ، عَرَضُوا عَلَيْهِمْ الْعَشَاءَ فَغَلَبُوهُمْ"، وَذَكَرَ الْحَدِيثَ.

وَفِي رِوَايَةٍ: {كَانَ يَتَحَدَّثُ إلَى النَّبِيِّ صَلَّى اللَّهُ عَلَيْهِ وَسَلَّمَ إلَى اللَّيْلِ}. وَفِي سَفَرِ الْهِجْرَةِ لَمْ يَصْحَبْهُ غَيْرُ أَبِي بَكْرٍ؛ وَيَوْمَ بَدْرٍ لَمْ يَبْقَ مَعَهُ فِي الْعَرِيشِ غَيْرُهُ. وَقَالَ: {إنَّ أَمَنَّ النَّاسِ عَلَيْنَا فِي صُحْبَتِهِ وَذَاتِ يَدِهِ أَبُو بَكْرٍ؛ وَلَوْ كُنْت مُتَّخِذًا مِنْ أَهْلِ الْأَرْضِ خَلِيلًا لَاتَّخَذْت أَبَا بَكْرٍ خَلِيلًا}. وَهَذَا مِنْ أَصَحِّ الْأَحَادِيثِ الْمُسْتَفِيضَةِ فِي الصِّحَاحِ مِنْ وُجُوهٍ كَثِيرَةٍ.

---

(*mutawātir*). See Minhāj al-Sunnah (4/28). The eleventh century scholar, ʿAlī ibn Ibrāhīm al-Ḥalabī, author of *al-Sīra al-Ḥalabiyya*, said, "This ḥadīth is authentic. It was reported from ten and some companions. Due to its abundant routes, it was listed among the mass-transmitted (*mutawātir*) traditions." See al-Sīra al-Ḥalabiyya (3/486).

In the *Ṣaḥīḥayn*, it is reported from Abū al-Dardāʾ that he said, "I was once seated with the Prophet ﷺ, and Abū Bakr approached, holding one end of his garment in such a way that his knee was exposed." Thereupon, the Prophet ﷺ commented, "As for your companion, he has preceded in goodness (*ghāmara*), so he was secured." Abū Bakr then said, "There was a quarrel between me and Ibn al-Khaṭṭāb, so I rushedly offended him. I then regretted that, so I asked him to forgive me, but he refused. Hence, I've come to you." The Prophet ﷺ then said, "May Allah forgive you," thrice. Later, ʿUmar regretted what he did, so he approached Abū Bakr's house, yet he did not find him. He then approached the Prophet ﷺ, and the Prophet's face became angered and furious such that even Abū Bakr felt sorry. Abū Bakr thus said, "I was more at fault, O Messenger of Allah," twice. The Prophet ﷺ then said, "Allah sent me to all of you, and you all impugned me, yet Abū Bakr trusted me! He consoled me with his life and wealth. Will you not let my companion be?! Will you not let my companion be?!" Abū Bakr was never harmed by anyone after that.(1) Al-Bukhārī said, "'*Ghāmara*' means to precede in goodness."

In the *Ṣaḥīḥayn*, it is reported from Ibn ʿAbbās that he said, "ʿUmar's body was laid on his bed, and the people engulfed him, supplicating for him, praising him, and praying for him before his body was transported. I was among them, and nothing surprised me except a man who had grabbed my shoulder from behind. I turned, and it was ʿAlī. He prayed for Allah's mercy on ʿUmar, and he said, 'Of all people, you are the one with whose good deeds I wish to face Allah most. By Allah, I had believed that Allah would place you among your two companions. That is because I used to frequently hear the Prophet say, 'Abū Bakr, ʿUmar and I came,' and 'Abū Bakr, ʿUmar and I entered,' and 'Abū Bakr, ʿUmar and I left.' I used to hope or expect that Allah would place you with them.'"(2)

---

(1) Ṣaḥīḥ al-Bukhārī (5/5)

(2) Ṣaḥīḥ al-Bukhārī (5/9-11), Ṣaḥīḥ Muslim (4/1858-1859)

وَفِي الصَّحِيحَيْنِ عَنْ أَبِي الدَّرْدَاءِ قَالَ: {كُنْتُ جَالِسًا عِنْدَ النَّبِيِّ ﷺ إِذْ أَقْبَلَ أَبُو بَكْرٍ آخِذًا بِطَرْفِ ثَوْبِهِ حَتَّى أَبْدَى عَنْ رُكْبَتِهِ، فَقَالَ النَّبِيُّ ﷺ: أَمَّا صَاحِبُكُمْ فَقَدْ غَامَرَ فَسَلَّمَ. وَقَالَ: إِنِّي كَانَ بَيْنِي وَبَيْنَ ابْنِ الْخَطَّابِ شَيْءٌ فَأَسْرَعْتُ إِلَيْهِ، ثُمَّ نَدِمْتُ فَسَأَلْتُهُ أَنْ يَغْفِرَ لِي فَأَبَى عَلَيَّ، فَأَتَيْتُكَ. فَقَالَ: يَغْفِرُ اللَّهُ لَكَ – ثَلَاثًا. ثُمَّ إِنَّ عُمَرَ نَدِمَ فَأَتَى مَنْزِلَ أَبِي بَكْرٍ فَلَمْ يَجِدْهُ، فَأَتَى النَّبِيَّ ﷺ فَجَعَلَ وَجْهُ النَّبِيِّ ﷺ يَتَمَعَّرُ وَغَضِبَ حَتَّى أَشْفَقَ أَبُو بَكْرٍ وَقَالَ: أَنَا كُنْتُ أَظْلَمَ يَا رَسُولَ اللَّهِ – مَرَّتَيْنِ. فَقَالَ النَّبِيُّ ﷺ: إِنَّ اللَّهَ بَعَثَنِي إِلَيْكُمْ فَقُلْتُمْ: كَذَبْتَ، وَقَالَ أَبُو بَكْرٍ: صَدَقْتَ. وَوَاسَانِي بِنَفْسِهِ وَمَالِهِ، فَهَلْ أَنْتُمْ تَارِكُوا لِي صَاحِبِي؟! فَهَلْ أَنْتُمْ تَارِكُوا لِي صَاحِبِي؟!}، فَمَا أُوذِيَ بَعْدَهَا. قَالَ الْبُخَارِيُّ: غَامَرَ: سَبَقَ بِالْخَيْرِ.

وَفِي الصَّحِيحَيْنِ عَنِ ابْنِ عَبَّاسٍ قَالَ: {وُضِعَ عُمَرُ عَلَى سَرِيرِهِ فَتَكَنَّفَهُ النَّاسُ يَدْعُونَ وَيُثْنُونَ وَيُصَلُّونَ عَلَيْهِ قَبْلَ أَنْ يُرْفَعَ، وَأَنَا فِيهِمْ. فَلَمْ يَرُعْنِي إِلَّا رَجُلٌ قَدْ أَخَذَ بِمَنْكِبِي مِنْ وَرَائِي، فَالْتَفَتُّ فَإِذَا هُوَ عَلِيٌّ. وَتَرَحَّمَ عَلَى عُمَرَ وَقَالَ: مَا خَلَّفْتَ أَحَدًا أَحَبَّ إِلَيَّ أَنْ أَلْقَى اللَّهَ عَزَّ وَجَلَّ بِعَمَلِهِ مِنْكَ، وَأَيْمُ اللَّهِ إِنْ كُنْتُ لَأَظُنُّ أَنْ يَجْعَلَكَ اللَّهُ مَعَ صَاحِبَيْكَ. وَذَلِكَ أَنِّي كُنْتُ كَثِيرًا مَا أَسْمَعُ النَّبِيَّ ﷺ يَقُولُ: "جِئْتُ أَنَا وَأَبُو بَكْرٍ وَعُمَرُ،" وَ"دَخَلْتُ أَنَا وَأَبُو بَكْرٍ وَعُمَرُ،" وَ"خَرَجْتُ أَنَا وَأَبُو بَكْرٍ وَعُمَرُ." فَإِنْ كُنْتُ أَرْجُو أَوْ أَظُنُّ أَنْ يَجْعَلَكَ اللَّهُ مَعَهُمَا}.

In the *Ṣaḥīḥayn* and other sources, it is reported that on the Day of Uḥud, when the Muslims were struck, Abū Sufyān said, "Is Muḥammad among the people? Is Muḥammad among the people? Is Muḥammad among the people?" In response, the Prophet ﷺ said, "Do not answer him." Abū Sufyān then said, "Is Ibn Abī Quḥāfa (Abū Bakr) among the people? Is Ibn Abī Quḥāfa (Abū Bakr) among the people? Is Ibn Abī Quḥāfa (Abū Bakr) among the people?" The Prophet ﷺ said to them, "Do not answer him." Abū Sufyān then said, "Is Ibn al-Khaṭṭāb among the people? Is Ibn al-Khaṭṭāb among the people? Is Ibn al-Khaṭṭāb among the people?" The Prophet ﷺ said to them, "Do not answer him." Abū Sufyān then said to his companions, "As for the aforementioned individuals, you have been sufficed of them." Unable to restrain himself, ʿUmar retorted, "You have lied, O enemy of Allah! The ones you named are still alive, and there remains more that will dismay you!"(1)

Here is the commander of the disbelievers in that state specifically inquiring about the Prophet ﷺ, Abū Bakr, and ʿUmar due to his awareness that they were the leaders of the Muslims: the Prophet ﷺ and his two aides.

For this reason, when [Hārūn] al-Rashīd inquired Mālik ibn Anas about Abū Bakr and ʿUmar's significance to the Prophet ﷺ during his lifetime, Mālik ibn Anas replied, "Their rank with respect to the Prophet ﷺ during his lifetime mirrors their rank with respect to him following his death."(2) Frequent companionship and priviness, paralleled with love, compassion, harmony, and sharing of knowledge and faith, entails that they both were more worthy of these things than others. This is apparent and evident to anyone with experience in those people's state of affairs.

---

(1) Ṣaḥīḥ al-Bukhārī (4/65, 5/94), Musnad Aḥmed ibn Ḥanbal (30/554-556)

(2) Kitāb al-Sharīʿa of al-ʾĀjurrī (5/2369-2370), Kitāb al-Mashyakha al-Kubrā of Qāḍī al-Māristān (2/410-411), Tārīkh Dimashq of Ibn ʿAsākir (30/396-397, 44/383)

وَفِي الصَّحِيحَيْنِ وَغَيْرِهِمَا أَنَّهُ {لَمَّا كَانَ يَوْمُ أُحُدٍ قَالَ أَبُو سُفْيَانَ لَمَّا أُصِيبَ الْمُسْلِمُونَ: "أَفِي الْقَوْمِ مُحَمَّدٌ؟ أَفِي الْقَوْمِ مُحَمَّدٌ؟ أَفِي الْقَوْمِ مُحَمَّدٌ؟" فَقَالَ النَّبِيُّ ﷺ: "لَا تُجِيبُوهُ." فَقَالَ: "أَفِي الْقَوْمِ ابْنُ أَبِي قُحَافَةَ؟ أَفِي الْقَوْمِ ابْنُ أَبِي قُحَافَةَ؟ أَفِي الْقَوْمِ ابْنُ أَبِي قُحَافَةَ؟" فَقَالَ النَّبِيُّ ﷺ: "لَا تُجِيبُوهُ." فَقَالَ: "أَفِي الْقَوْمِ ابْنُ الْخَطَّابِ؟ أَفِي الْقَوْمِ ابْنُ الْخَطَّابِ؟ أَفِي الْقَوْمِ ابْنُ الْخَطَّابِ؟" فَقَالَ النَّبِيُّ ﷺ: "لَا تُجِيبُوهُ." فَقَالَ لِأَصْحَابِهِ: "أَمَّا هَؤُلَاءِ فَقَدْ كَفَيْتُمُوهُمْ." فَلَمْ يَمْلِكْ عُمَرُ نَفْسَهُ أَنْ قَالَ: "كَذَبْتَ عَدُوَّ اللَّهِ! إِنَّ الَّذِينَ عَدَدْتَ لَأَحْيَاءٌ، وَقَدْ بَقِيَ لَكَ مَا يَسُوءُكَ!"} الْحَدِيثَ.

فَهَذَا أَمِيرُ الْكُفَّارِ فِي تِلْكَ الْحَالِ إِنَّمَا سَأَلَ عَنِ النَّبِيِّ ﷺ وَأَبِي بَكْرٍ وَعُمَرَ دُونَ غَيْرِهِمْ لِعِلْمِهِ بِأَنَّهُمْ رُءُوسُ الْمُسْلِمِينَ: النَّبِيُّ وَوَزِيرَاهُ.

وَلِهَذَا سَأَلَ الرَّشِيدُ مَالِكَ بْنَ أَنَسٍ عَنْ مَنْزِلَتِهِمَا مِنَ النَّبِيِّ ﷺ فِي حَيَاتِهِ فَقَالَ: مَنْزِلَتُهُمَا مِنْهُ فِي حَيَاتِهِ كَمَنْزِلَتِهِمَا مِنْهُ بَعْدَ مَمَاتِهِ. وَكَثْرَةُ الِاخْتِصَاصِ وَالصُّحْبَةِ – مَعَ كَمَالِ الْمَوَدَّةِ وَالِائْتِلَافِ وَالْمَحَبَّةِ وَالْمُشَارَكَةِ فِي الْعِلْمِ وَالدِّينِ – تَقْتَضِي أَنَّهُمَا أَحَقُّ بِذَلِكَ مِنْ غَيْرِهِمَا. وَهَذَا ظَاهِرٌ بَيِّنٌ لِمَنْ لَهُ خِبْرَةٌ بِأَحْوَالِ الْقَوْمِ.

Regarding al-Ṣiddīq, besides his upholding of several matters of knowledge and *fiqh* that others failed to uphold, thereby elucidating them, he also has no recorded opinions that contradicted proof-texts. This attests to his utmost excellence. In contrast, there exist many opinions recorded from other than Abū Bakr that conflict with proof-texts, as those proof-texts (*nuṣūṣ*) did not reach those individuals.

As for ʿUmar, his opinions that were found aligned with the proof-texts (*nuṣūṣ*) outnumber those of ʿAlī. This is known to anyone well-versed in the matters of law and the positions held by the respective scholars. An example is the widow's alimony: ʿUmar's position is the one that was aligned with the *naṣṣ*, as opposed to the latter position. Similar to that is the issue of *ḥarām*: the position held by ʿUmar and others more closely reflects the proof-texts (*nuṣūṣ*) compared to the other position.[1]

It is established in the *Ṣaḥīḥayn* that the Prophet ﷺ said, "In the nations before you, there were inspired individuals. If such an individual exists in my nation, then it would be ʿUmar."[2]

---

(1) Ibn Taymiyya's point here is precisely articulated. He is not arguing that one position is blatantly fallacious while the other is patently correct. Rather, he is stating that one of them is better aligned with the proof-texts than the other. That is because the disputed matter is not explicitly addressed in any prophetic traditions or Quranic verses, and both positions are based on legal analogies (*qiyās*).

The disputed matter is the ruling of a man who tells his wife, "You are now *ḥarām* to me." ʿUmar ibn al-Khaṭṭāb held that this statement is akin to an oath (*yamīn*), which means that a man in such a situation can break the oath and pay the penalty (*kaffāra*) of breaking the oath while remaining lawfully married to his wife. See Muṣannaf ʿAbdirrazzāq (6/399-400) and Sunan Saʿīd ibn Manṣūr (1/436).

ʿUmar's position is also the position of several Ṣaḥāba, including Ibn ʿAbbās, who drew an analogy between it and another precedent set by the Messenger of Allah; see Ṣaḥīḥ al-Bukhārī (6/156) and Ṣaḥīḥ Muslim (2/1100). Alī, on the other hand, considered such a statement equivalent to a triple divorce. See Muṣannaf ʿAbdirrazzāq (6/403).

(2) Ṣaḥīḥ al-Bukhārī (4/174, 5/12), Ṣaḥīḥ Muslim (1/1864)

أَمَّا الصِّدِّيقُ فَإِنَّهُ مَعَ قِيَامِهِ بِأُمُورٍ مِنْ الْعِلْمِ وَالْفِقْهِ عَجزَ عَنْهَا غَيْرُهُ - حَتَّى بَيَّنَهَا لَهُمْ - لَمْ يُحْفَظْ لَهُ قَوْلٌ مُخَالِفٌ نَصًّا. هَذَا يَدُلُّ عَلَى غَايَةِ الْبَرَاعَةِ. وَأَمَّا غَيْرُهُ فَحُفِظَتْ لَهُ أَقْوَالٌ كَثِيرَةٌ خَالَفَتْ النَّصَّ لِكَوْنِ تِلْكَ النُّصُوصِ لَمْ تَبْلُغْهُمْ.

وَالَّذِي وُجِدَ مِنْ مُوَافَقَةِ عُمَرَ لِلنُّصُوصِ أَكْثَرُ مِنْ مُوَافَقَةِ عَلِيٍّ. وَهَذَا يَعْرِفُهُ مَنْ عَرَفَ مَسَائِلَ الْعِلْمِ وَأَقْوَالَ الْعُلَمَاءِ فِيهَا. وَذَلِكَ مِثْلُ نَفَقَةِ الْمُتَوَفَّى عَنْهَا زَوْجُهَا، فَإِنَّ قَوْلَ عُمَرَ هُوَ الَّذِي وَافَقَ النَّصَّ دُونَ الْقَوْلِ الْآخَرِ. وَكَذَلِكَ مَسْأَلَةُ الْحَرَامِ قَوْلُ عُمَرَ وَغَيْرِهِ فِيهَا هُوَ الْأَشْبَهُ بِالنُّصُوصِ مِنْ الْقَوْلِ الْآخَرِ.

وَقَدْ ثَبَتَ فِي الصَّحِيحَيْنِ عَنْ النَّبِيِّ ﷺ أَنَّهُ قَالَ: {قَدْ كَانَ فِي الْأُمَمِ قَبْلَكُمْ مُحَدَّثُونَ فَإِنْ يَكُنْ فِي أُمَّتِي أَحَدٌ فَعُمَرُ}.

In the *Ṣaḥīḥayn*, it is reported from the Prophet ﷺ that he said, "I dreamt that I was given a cup of milk. I drank from it, and I could observe the nourishment coming out of my fingernails. I then passed the remaining milk to ʿUmar." Those present thus inquired, "How did you interpret this dream, O Messenger of Allah?" He replied, "Knowledge."(1)

In al-Tirmiḏī and others, it is reported that the Prophet ﷺ said, "Had I not been sent to you, then ʿUmar would have been sent."(2)

Furthermore, the Prophet ﷺ, in his absence, designated al-Ṣiddīq to lead prayer,(3) which is the pillar of Islam, and [he designated him] to uphold the rites of *Ḥajj*, which are some of the most convoluted matters of worship.(4) Abū Bakr led the rites of *Ḥajj* prior to the Prophet's ﷺ pilgrimage, and he called out, "No polytheist shall perform pilgrimage after this year, and no nude person shall circumambulate around the House!" The Prophet ﷺ then sent ʿAlī in his trail to annul the pact with the polytheists. Upon ʿAlī's arrival to Abū Bakr, Abū Bakr inquired, "[Were you sent] as a superior or as a subordinate?" ʿAlī replied, "As a subordinate."(5)

---

(1) Ṣaḥīḥ al-Bukhārī (1/27-28, 5/10, 9/35), Ṣaḥīḥ Muslim (4/1859-1860)

(2) Al-Jāmiʿ al-Kabīr of al-Tirmiḏī (6/59-60). Imām Aḥmed ibn Ḥanbal disapproved of this tradition. See al-Muntakhab Min ʿIlal al-Khallāl (p. 190-191). The ḥadīth may be a mutation of the earlier established ḥadīth about ʿUmar potentially being inspired.

(3) Ṣaḥīḥ al-Bukhārī (1/133-134, 1/136-137), Ṣaḥīḥ Muslim (1/313-316)

(4) Ṣaḥīḥ al-Bukhārī (2/153), Ṣaḥīḥ Muslim (2/982), Ṣaḥīḥ Ibn Khuzayma (p. 674), Ṣaḥīḥ Ibn Ḥibbān (4/192)

(5) Al-Sīra al-Nabawiyya of ibn Hishām (2/461). This is an interesting reference which illustrates Ibn Taymiyya's impressive employment of a wide array of sources to substantiate his case. In this instance, he is referencing Ibn Isḥāq's account, which is quite an early source. While Ibn Isḥāq does not list an isnād for this report, it is quite noteworthy how ʿAlī's subordinancy to Abū Bakr is explicitly mentioned in this early text.

وَفِي الصَّحِيحَيْنِ عَنْ النَّبِيِّ ﷺ أَنَّهُ قَالَ: {رَأَيْت كَأَنِّي أُتِيت بِقَدَحِ لَبَنٍ فَشَرِبْت حَتَّى أَنِّي لَأَرَى الرِّيَّ يَخْرُجُ مِنْ أَظْفَارِي، ثُمَّ نَاوَلْت فَضْلِي عُمَرَ. فَقَالُوا: مَا أَوَّلْته يَا رَسُولَ اللَّهِ؟ قَالَ: الْعِلْمُ}.

وَفِي التِّرْمِذِيِّ وَغَيْرِهِ أَنَّهُ قَالَ: {لَوْ لَمْ أُبْعَثْ فِيكُمْ لَبُعِثَ عُمَرُ} .

وَأَيْضًا فَإِنَّ الصِّدِّيقَ اسْتَخْلَفَهُ النَّبِيُّ ﷺ عَلَى الصَّلَاةِ الَّتِي هِيَ عَمُودُ الْإِسْلَامِ وَعَلَى إقَامَةِ الْمَنَاسِكِ الَّتِي لَيْسَ فِي مَسَائِلِ الْعِبَادَاتِ أَشْكَلُ مِنْهَا. وَأَقَامَ الْمَنَاسِكَ قَبْلَ أَنْ يَحُجَّ النَّبِيُّ ﷺ فَنَادَى أَنْ لَا يَحُجَّ بَعْدَ الْعَامِ مُشْرِكٌ وَلَا يَطُوفَ بِالْبَيْتِ عُرْيَانُ. فَأَرْدَفَهُ بِعَلِيِّ بْنِ أَبِي طَالِبٍ لِيَنْبِذَ الْعَهْدَ إلَى الْمُشْرِكِينَ، فَلَمَّا لَحِقَهُ قَالَ: أَمِيرٌ أَوْ مَأْمُورٌ؟ قَالَ: بَلْ مَأْمُورٌ.

---

A host of other traditions similarly present Abū Bakr being appointed to lead the rites of Ḥajj. Elsewhere, Ibn Taymiyya elaborates, "It is known and mass-transmitted (*mutawātir*) among the scholars of *Tafsīr*, *Maghāzī*, *Siyar*, *Ḥadīth*, *Fiqh*, and others that the Prophet appointed Abū Bakr to lead the Ḥajj in year 9..." See Minhāj al-Sunnah of Ibn Taymiyya (5/490).

Perhaps a brief pause here is warranted for reflection and contemplation. Twelver polemicists, in their attempt to validate certain dubious historical claims pivotal to the Twelver narrative, will often argue that historical reports should not undergo the same rigorous scrutiny as ḥadīths pertaining to jurisprudence and theology. This standard, however, is selectively applied by such Twelver polemicists with traditions that support Twelver preconceptions and beliefs. Should they remain consistent in this approach with weak historical traditions found in works like the *Sīra* of Ibn Isḥāq and others, a Twelver interpretation of history simply would be untenable. Such polemicists effectively seek to have their cake and eat it with a select subgroup of weak traditions more closely aligned with Twelver dogma.

The Prophet ﷺ thus placed Abū Bakr in-charge of ʿAlī ibn Abī Ṭālib, and ʿAlī was among those who were instructed by the Prophet ﷺ to obey and listen to Abū Bakr concerning *Ḥajj*, the rulings pertaining the travelers, and other matters. This came after the expedition of Tabūk when the Prophet ﷺ entrusted ʿAlī with leadership of Medīna in his absence.(1) At the time, the only men left in Medīna were either hypocrites, those with valid excuses, or sinners. ʿAlī thus pursued the Prophet ﷺ and said, "Do you leave me behind with the women and children?!" The Prophet ﷺ replied, "Are you not content in being to me as Aaron was to Moses?"(2)

---

(1) Whether ʿAlī was even designated as governor of Medina during the Expedition of Tabūk or not is a matter of dispute among the early historions.

Ibn Isḥāq, Ibn Hishām and Ibn Saʿd stated that Muḥammad ibn Maslama al-Anṣārī was left in charge of Medīna during the Expedition of Tabūk. See al-Sīra al-Nabawiyya of Ibn Hishām (2/440), Tārikh Dimashq (2/31), and Kitāb al-Ṭabaqāt al-Kabīr of Ibn Saʿd (2/151). Al-Wāqidī also reported an account explicitly affirming this position; see Kitāb al-Ṭabaqāt al-Kabīr of Ibn Saʿd (3/409). This position was chosen by a host of later scholars. Ibn Isḥāq elaborated that ʿAlī was specifically left behind to tend and care for the Prophet's family and dependents.

The *tābiʿī*, al-Shaʿbī, reported that Ibn Um Maktūm was designed as the governor of Medina at the time, and this is one of the positions recorded from al-Wāqidī. See Muṣannaf ʿAbdirrazzāq (2/395) and Kitāb al-Maghāzī of al-Wāqidī (p. 43).

Al-Darāwardī's father stated that it was Sibāʿ ibn Urfuṭa who was left in charge of the city at the time, and this is one of the positions recorded from al-Wāqidī. See al-Sīra al-Nabawiyya of Ibn Hishām (2/440) and Kitāb al-Maghāzī of al-Wāqidī (p. 659). Khalīfa ibn Khayyāṭ also held this position; see Tārīkh Khalīfa ibn Khayyāṭ (p. 97).

The Mutazilite scholar, al-Jāḥiẓ, elaborated, "Even if they disagreed [on the identity of Medina's governor during the Expedition of Tabūk], they are in agreement that ʿAlī was in Medina whilst the governor was someone else." See al-ʿUthmāniyya of al-Jāḥiẓ (p. 153). It should be noted, however, that a variety of scholars understood from the traditions that ʿAlī was was the Messenger of Allah's governor in Medina during Tabūk. I merely expound this section to highlight the existence of disagreement among the early historians in this regard.

(2) Ṣaḥīḥ al-Bukhārī (6/3), Ṣaḥīḥ Muslim (4/1870)

فَأَمَّرَ أَبَا بَكْرٍ عَلَى عَلِيِّ بْنِ أَبِي طَالِبٍ، وَكَانَ عَلِيٌّ مِمَّنْ أَمَّرَهُ النَّبِيُّ ﷺ أَنْ يَسْمَعَ وَيُطِيعَ فِي الْحَجِّ وَأَحْكَامِ الْمُسَافِرِينَ وَغَيْرِ ذَلِكَ لِأَبِي بَكْرٍ، وَكَانَ هَذَا بَعْدَ غَزْوَةِ تَبُوكَ الَّتِي اسْتَخْلَفَ عَلِيًّا فِيهَا عَلَى الْمَدِينَةِ. وَلَمْ يَكُنْ بَقِيَ بِالْمَدِينَةِ مِنَ الرِّجَالِ إِلَّا مُنَافِقٌ أَوْ مَعْذُورٌ أَوْ مُذْنِبٌ، فَلَحِقَهُ عَلِيٌّ فَقَالَ: "أَتُخَلِّفُنِي مَعَ النِّسَاءِ وَالصِّبْيَانِ؟!" فَقَالَ: "أَمَا تَرْضَى أَنْ تَكُونَ مِنِّي بِمَنْزِلَةِ هَارُونَ مِنْ مُوسَى؟"

In that statement, he clarified that leaving him behind in-charge of Medīna was not a reflection of any diminished status, for Moses had left Aaron behind in-charge.(1) The Prophet ﷺ used to deputize men in his absence, but other men usually remained in Medina [in such instances]. In the year of Tabūk, the Prophet ﷺ mobilized alongside him all Muslims without exception. He gave no one permission to forsake the expedition because the enemy was formidable and the journey was distant. It was during this expedition that Allah revealed *Sūrat Barāʾa.*

Abū Bakr's document on *zakat* (*ṣadaqāt*) is the most comprehensive and concise of documents, which is why most of the jurists adopted it. As for the latter's document, it contains things that were early and abrogated, and that is evidence that Abū Bakr is more knowledgeable in the abrogative *Sunnah.* (2)

---

(1) Perhaps it may also be added here: if the historians who held that a man other than ʿAlī was the governor of Medina during the Expedition of Tabūk, then it would further highlight Shi'ite misuse and misinterpretation of this tradition as an announcement of ʿAlī's successorship.

(2) Ibn Taymiyya, in *Minhāj al-Sunnah*, elaborated, saying, "The most correct of them according to the Muslim scholars is the book of Abū Bakr that he wrote to Anas ibn Mālik, and it is the one reported by al-Bukhārī and acted upon by most of the *Imāms.* After it in ranking is ʿUmar's book. As for the book reported from ʿAlī, it contains things that were not upheld by any of the scholars, such as his statement, 'For 25 [camels], five sheep [are owed].' This is contrary to the mass-trasnmitter (*mutawātira*) proof-texts from the Prophet. For this reason, what was reported from ʿAlī in this regard was either abrogated or an error in transmission." See Minhāj al-Sunnah al-Nabawiyya (8/279-280).

As for ʿAlī's document referenced by Ibn Taymiyya, it is reported through ʿĀṣim ibn Ḍamra, from ʿAlī ibn Abī Ṭālib. See Muṣannaf Ibn Abī Shayba (6/396) and Muṣannaf ʿAbdirrazzāq (4/5).

The scholar, al-Qāsim ibn Sallām, commented on the problematized clause from ʿAlī's tradition, saying, "No one from the people of Hejaz, Iraq, or anyone else we know acted upon this. It was reported from Sufyān ibn Saʿīd that he used to deny that this is from ʿAlī's speech, and he would say, "ʿAlī was more knowledgeble than to utter that.'" See Kitāb al-Amwāl of Abū ʿUbayd al-Qāsim ibn Sallām (2/10-11).

بَيَّنَ بِذَلِكَ أَنَّ اسْتِخْلَافَ عَلِيٍّ عَلَى الْمَدِينَةِ لَا يَقْتَضِي نَقْصَ الْمَرْتَبَةِ، فَإِنَّ مُوسَى قَدْ اسْتَخْلَفَ هَارُونَ. وَكَانَ النَّبِيُّ ﷺ دَائِمًا يَسْتَخْلِفُ رِجَالًا، لَكِنْ كَانَ يَكُونُ بِهَا رِجَالٌ. وَعَامَ تَبُوكَ خَرَجَ النَّبِيُّ ﷺ بِجَمِيعِ الْمُسْلِمِينَ وَلَمْ يَأْذَنْ لِأَحَدٍ فِي التَّخَلُّفِ عَنْ الْغُزَاةِ، لِأَنَّ الْعَدُوَّ كَانَ شَدِيدًا وَالسَّفَرُ بَعِيدًا، وَفِيهَا أَنْزَلَ اللَّهُ سُورَةَ بَرَاءَةٌ.

وَكِتَابُ أَبِي بَكْرٍ فِي الصَّدَقَاتِ أَجْمَعُ الْكُتُبِ وَأَوْجَزُهَا، وَلِهَذَا عَمِلَ بِهِ عَامَّةُ الْفُقَهَاءِ. وَكِتَابُ غَيْرِهِ فِيهِ مَا هُوَ مُتَقَدِّمٌ مَنْسُوخٌ، فَدَلَّ ذَلِكَ عَلَى أَنَّهُ أَعْلَمُ بِالسُّنَّةِ النَّاسِخَةِ.

---

This ḥadīth may thus prove to be an error in transmission from ʿAlī or an error in *ijtihad* on his part. What is telling, however, is that Twelver Shi'ites today actually uphold this patently incorrect position that is ascribed to ʿAlī, which is that five sheep are owed with possession of 25 camels, so Ibn Taymiyya's argument is potent regardless. The Twelver scholar, al-Sharīf al-Murtaḍā, claimed that there was a consensus within the Twelver sect to adopt this position on *zakat* and that it was a unique position of the Imāmīs. See al-Intiṣār of al-Sharīf al-Murtaḍā (p. 80-81).

In the *Ṣaḥīḥayn*, it is reported from Abū Saʿīd that he said, "And Abū Bakr was the most knowledgeable of us in the Messenger of Allah ﷺ."(1)

Furthermore, whenever the *Ṣaḥāba* disagreed on a matter during Abū Bakr's reign, Abū Bakr would settle it, resolving the dispute. Every disputed matter among them during Abū Bakr's reign was resolved because of him. An example is their dispute regarding the Prophet's ﷺ death, burial and inheritance; and regarding the preparation of Usāma's army; and his combat of those who withheld *zakat*; and other great matters.

The Prophet's *Khalīfa* (successor) was with them, educating them, rectifying them, and elucidating to them such that any confusion was dissipated. They did not used to dispute Abū Bakr's views. After Abū Bakr, no one matched him in knowledge and excellence, and they consequently disputed some matters among themselves. An example is their dispute regarding [the inheritance] of a grandfather and siblings, *Ḥarām*, triple divorce, and other known matters that were uncontested during Abū Bakr's reign.

They used to contest many of ʿUmar, ʿUthmān, and ʿAlī's opinions, but it is not known that they ever contested any of Abū Bakr's adjudications or legal opinions. This is evidence of his utmost knowledge.

He stood in the Prophet's place and upheld Islam, not falling short in any of it. In fact, he managed to guide people back [into Islam] through the very door they had once exited it. He accomplished this despite the abundance of dissidents from the apostates and others and the abundance of forsakers. Through him, their knowledge and faith was sufficed such that none resisted him, and the faith became upright as it previously was.

---

(1) Ṣaḥīḥ al-Bukhārī (5/57-58), Ṣaḥīḥ Muslim (4/1854)

وَفِي الصَّحِيحَيْنِ عَنْ أَبِي سَعِيدٍ، قَالَ: "وَكَانَ أَبُو بَكْرٍ أَعْلَمَنَا بِرَسُولِ اللَّهِ ﷺ."

وَأَيْضًا فَالصَّحَابَةُ فِي زَمَنِ أَبِي بَكْرٍ لَمْ يَكُونُوا يَتَنَازَعُونَ فِي مَسْأَلَةٍ إِلَّا فَصَلَهَا بَيْنَهُمْ أَبُو بَكْرٍ وَارْتَفَعَ النِّزَاعُ. فَلَا يُعْرَفُ بَيْنَهُمْ فِي زَمَانِهِ مَسْأَلَةٌ وَاحِدَةٌ تَنَازَعُوا فِيهَا إِلَّا ارْتَفَعَ النِّزَاعُ بَيْنَهُمْ بِسَبَبِهِ، كَتَنَازُعِهِمْ فِي وَفَاتِهِ ﷺ وَمَدْفِنِهِ وَفِي مِيرَاثِهِ وَفِي تَجْهِيزِ جَيْشِ أُسَامَةَ وَقِتَالِ مَانِعِي الزَّكَاةِ؛ وَغَيْرِ ذَلِكَ مِنَ الْمَسَائِلِ الْكِبَارِ.

بَلْ كَانَ خَلِيفَةَ رَسُولِ اللَّهِ ﷺ فِيهِمْ يُعَلِّمُهُمْ وَيُقَوِّمُهُمْ وَيُبَيِّنُ لَهُمْ مَا تَزُولُ مَعَهُ الشُّبْهَةُ، فَلَمْ يَكُونُوا مَعَهُ يَخْتَلِفُونَ. وَبَعْدَهُ لَمْ يَبْلُغْ عِلْمُ أَحَدٍ وَكَمَالُهُ عِلْمَ أَبِي بَكْرٍ وَكَمَالَهُ. فَصَارُوا يَتَنَازَعُونَ فِي بَعْضِ الْمَسَائِلِ، كَمَا تَنَازَعُوا فِي الْجَدِّ وَالْإِخْوَةِ وَفِي الْحَرَامِ وَفِي الطَّلَاقِ الثَّلَاثِ؛ وَفِي غَيْرِ ذَلِكَ مِنَ الْمَسَائِلِ الْمَعْرُوفَةِ مِمَّا لَمْ يَكُونُوا يَتَنَازَعُونَ فِيهِ عَلَى عَهْدِ أَبِي بَكْرٍ.

وَكَانُوا يُخَالِفُونَ عُمَرَ وَعُثْمَانَ وَعَلِيًّا فِي كَثِيرٍ مِنْ أَقْوَالِهِمْ، وَلَمْ يُعْرَفْ أَنَّهُمْ خَالَفُوا أَبَا بَكْرٍ فِي شَيْءٍ مِمَّا كَانَ يُفْتِي فِيهِ وَيَقْضِي. وَهَذَا يَدُلُّ عَلَى غَايَةِ الْعِلْمِ.

وَقَامَ مَقَامَ رَسُولِ اللَّهِ ﷺ وَأَقَامَ الْإِسْلَامَ، فَلَمْ يُخِلَّ بِشَيْءٍ مِنْهُ. بَلْ أَدْخَلَ النَّاسَ مِنَ الْبَابِ الَّذِي خَرَجُوا مِنْهُ مَعَ كَثْرَةِ الْمُخَالِفِينَ مِنَ الْمُرْتَدِّينَ وَغَيْرِهِمْ وَكَثْرَةِ الْخَاذِلِينَ. فَكَمُلَ بِهِ مِنْ عِلْمِهِمْ وَدِينِهِمْ مَا لَا يُقَاوِمُهُ فِيهِ أَحَدٌ حَتَّى قَامَ الدِّينُ كَمَا كَانَ.

They referred to Abū Bakr as, "The Messenger of Allah's successor (*Khalīfatu Rasūlillāh*)."(1) Later, they referred to ʿUmar and others, "The Commander of the Faithful (*Amīr al-Muʾminīn*)."(2)

Al-Suhaylī and other scholars mentioned that the Prophet's ﷺ statement, "Do not worry, for Allah is with us [Quran 9:40]," was exhibited in Abū Bakr literally as it was figuratively. The people would frequently say, "The Messenger of Allah Muḥammad ﷺ and Abū Bakr, the Messenger of Allah's successor (*Khalīfatu Rasūlillāh*)." However, this nominal connection ceased after Abū Bakr's death, and they did not refer to anyone after Abū Bakr as "The Messenger of Allah's successor (*Khalīfat Rasūl-illāh*)."(3)

Moreover, ʿAlī ibn Abī Ṭālib had learned some of the *Sunnah* from Abū Bakr, while the reverse is not true, as Abū Bakr did not learn from ʿAlī ibn Abī Ṭālib. As is documented in the famous ḥadīth in the *Sunan*, which is the ḥadīth of the prayer of repentance, ʿAlī said, "Whenever I heard a ḥadīth directly from the Prophet ﷺ, Allah would let me benefit from it however He willed. However, if anyone else informed me of something, I would make them swear an oath [for validation]. If they swear, I would believe them. Abū Bakr informed me – and truthful was he – from the Prophet ﷺ that he said, 'Any Muslim who commits a sin, then performs *wuḍūʾ* properly, prays two *rakʿas*, asking Allah for forgiveness, then Allah shall forgive him.'"(4)

---

(1) Muṣannaf ʿAbdirrazzāq (10/275), Muṣannaf Ibn Abī Shayba (10/175, 10/349, 13/179, 19/137, 20/579-580, 20/585-586), Musnad Aḥmed ibn Ḥanbal (1/226, 1/241, 1/369)

(2) See Kitāb al-Ṭabaqāt al-Kabīr of Ibn Saʿd (3/262), Tārīkh al-Madīna of Ibn Shabba (2/678)

(3) Al-Rawḍ al-ʾUnuf of al-Suhaylī (4/216-217)

(4) Al-Jāmiʿ al-Kabīr of al-Tirmiḏī (1/431), Ṣaḥīḥ Ibn Ḥibbān (1/407)

وَكَانُوا يُسَمَّوْنَ أَبَا بَكْر خَلِيفَةَ رَسُولِ اللَّهِ ﷺ، ثُمَّ بَعْدَ هَذَا سَمَّوْا عُمَرَ وَغَيْرَهُ: أَمِيرَ الْمُؤْمِنِينَ.

قَالَ السهيلي وَغَيْرُهُ مِنْ الْعُلَمَاءِ: ظَهَرَ قَوْلُهُ: {لَا تَحْزَنْ إِنَّ اللَّهَ مَعَنَا} فِي أَبِي بَكْرٍ: فِي اللَّفْظِ كَمَا ظَهَرَ فِي الْمَعْنَى. فَكَانُوا يَقُولُونَ: "مُحَمَّدٌ رَسُولُ اللَّهِ وَأَبُو بَكْرٍ خَلِيفَةُ رَسُولِ اللَّهِ." ثُمَّ انْقَطَعَ هَذَا الِاتِّصَالُ اللَّفْظِيُّ بِمَوْتِهِ، فَلَمْ يَقُولُوا لِمَنْ بَعْده: "خَلِيفَةُ رَسُولِ اللَّهِ."

وَأَيْضًا فَعَلِيُّ بْنُ أَبِي طَالِبٍ تَعَلَّمَ مِنْ أَبِي بَكْرٍ بَعْضَ السُّنَّةِ، بِخِلَافِ أَبِي بَكْرٍ فَإِنَّهُ لَمْ يَتَعَلَّمْ مِنْ عَلِيِّ بْنِ أَبِي طَالِبٍ. كَمَا فِي الْحَدِيثِ الْمَشْهُورِ الَّذِي فِي السُّنَنِ حَدِيثِ صَلَاةِ التَّوْبَةِ عَنْ عَلِيٍّ، قَالَ: "كُنْت إذَا سَمِعْت مِنْ النَّبِيِّ ﷺ حَدِيثًا يَنْفَعُنِي اللَّهُ مِنْهُ بِمَا شَاءَ أَنْ يَنْفَعَنِي، فَإِذَا حَدَّثَنِي غَيْرُهُ اسْتَحْلَفْته، فَإِذَا حَلَفَ لِي صَدَّقْته، وَحَدَّثَنِي أَبُو بَكْرٍ – وَصَدَقَ أَبُو بَكْرٍ – عَنْ النَّبِيِّ ﷺ أَنَّهُ قَالَ {مَا مِنْ مُسْلِمٍ يُذْنِبُ ذَنْبًا ثُمَّ يَتَوَضَّأُ وَيُحْسِنُ الْوُضُوءَ وَيُصَلِّي رَكْعَتَيْنِ وَيَسْتَغْفِرُ اللَّهَ إلَّا غَفَرَ اللَّهُ لَهُ} ".

This is further demonstrated in how the *imāms* from Kufa's scholars who accompanied both, ʿUmar and ʿAlī, such as ʿAlqama, al-Aswad, Shurayḥ al-Qāḍī, and others, used to prioritize ʿUmar's opinions over ʿAlī's.(1) As for the *tābiʿīn* of Mecca, Medīna, and Baṣra, this is even more apparent and well-known among them, and it goes without saying.(2) As for Kufa, ʿAlī's *fiqh* and knowledge manifested within it proportionally to his residence there during his caliphate. It is unknown that anyone from ʿAlī's partisans who accompanied him ranked him above Abū Bakr and ʿUmar in terms of *fiqh*, knowledge, or other matters.

---

(1) This is unsurprising, given that al-Aswad and ʿAlqama were some of ʿAbdullāh ibn Masʿūd's most intimate disciples. Ibn Masʿūd used to say, "ʿUmar was the most knowledgeable among us in Allah, most recightful of Allah's Book, and of most *fiqh* in Allah's religion." Ibn Masʿūd also used to say, "By Allah, I suppose there is angel in between his eyes guiding him and directing him to the correct position." Ibn Masʿūd also used to say, "If the knowledge of all Arab tribes were placed on one end of a scale and ʿUmar's knowledge were placed on the other end, then the scale would have tipped in favor of ʿUmar's knowledge." See Muṣannaf Ibn Abī Shayba (17/55-57, 17/65).

As for Shurayḥ, he was appointed as a judge by ʿUmar himself, and it is rather apparent that ʿUmar was a major, if not primary, influence on him in terms of adjudication and related matters. See Muṣannaf Ibn Abī Shayba (3/261, 9/165, 9/168, 9/454, 10/154, 11/188-189, 11/503, 11/538, 11/606-607, 14/85, 16/336); and see Muṣannaf ʿAbdirrazzāq (5/195, 7/100, 8/24, 8/125, 9/345, 9/384-385, 9/394, 10/76-77, 10/299-300)

(2) A comprehensive analysis of early Hejazi ḥadīth collections, such as the *Muwaṭṭaʾ* of Imām Mālik the *Juzʾ* of Ismāʿīl ibn Jaʿfar and other texts, should demonstrate that ʿUmar ibn al-Khaṭṭāb's *fiqh* maintained a greater presence and relevance than that of ʿAlī (Allah be pleased with them both) in early Hejazi circles, though ʿAlī's *fiqh* maintained a presence therein as well. Elsewhere, Ibn Taymiyya elaborates, "For this reason, the people of Medina used to lean more closely towards ʿUmar's opinions, and their *maḏhab* is more preponderant than the *maḏhabs* of the (other) regions. No inhabitants of any Islamic city in the first three generations were more knowledgeable than them in the Messenger of Allah's *Sunnah*, and they agree in prioritizing ʿUmar's opinions over ʿAlī's." See Minhāj al-Sunnah (6/57).

Imām Mālik said, "I have not encountered anyone that I emulate doubting Abū Bakr and ʿUmar's precedence." See Musnad al-Muwaṭṭaʾ (p. 110).

وَمِمَّا يُبَيِّنُ لك هَذَا أَنَّ أَئِمَّةَ عُلَمَاءِ الْكُوفَةِ الَّذِينَ صَحِبُوا عُمَرَ وَعَلِيًّا كعلقمة وَالْأَسْوَدِ وشريح الْقَاضِي وَغَيْرِهِمْ كَانُوا يُرَجِّحُونَ قَوْلَ عُمَر عَلَى قَوْلِ عَلِيٍّ. وَأَمَّا تَابِعُوا أَهْلَ الْمَدِينَةِ وَمَكَّةَ وَالْبَصْرَةِ فَهَذَا عِنْدَهُمْ أَظْهَرُ وَأَشْهَرُ مِنْ أَنْ يُذْكَرَ. وَإِنَّمَا الْكُوفَةُ ظَهَرَ فِيهَا فِقْهُ عَلِيٍّ وَعِلْمُهُ بِحَسَبِ مَقَامِهِ فِيهَا مُدَّةَ خِلَافَتِهِ. وَكُلُّ شِيعَةِ عَلِيٍّ الَّذِينَ صَحِبُوهُ لَا يُعْرَفُ عَنْ أَحَدٍ مِنْهُمْ أَنَّهُ قَدَّمَهُ عَلَى أَبِي بَكْرٍ وَعُمَرَ لَا فِي فِقْهٍ وَلَا عِلْمٍ وَلَا غَيْرِهِمَا.

Indeed, all of ʿAlī's Shia who had fought his enemies by his side aligned with the rest of the Muslims in giving precedence to Abū Bakr and ʿUmar, save for those whom ʿAlī denounced and criticized, who were sparse and insignificant during his reign.

They (the Shia) were three factions. One group held extremist beliefs about ʿAlī, such as the group that believed in his divinity, and ʿAlī incinerated them with fire.(1) Another faction used to disparage Abū Bakr, and their leader was ʿAbdullāh ibn Sabaʾ. Upon learning of this, ʿAlī sought to kill him, but ʿAbdullāh managed to escape. (2) There was a third faction that used to give precedence to him over Abū Bakr and ʿUmar, to which ʿAlī said, "Should I learn that any of you ranks me above Abū Bakr and ʿUmar, then I will flog him as I flog a slanderer."(3)

It has been reported from ʿAlī through more than 80 routes that he said whilst on the pulpit of Kufa, "The best from this *Ummah* after its Prophet ﷺ are Abū Bakr and ʿUmar."(4)

---

(1) Ṣaḥīḥ al-Bukhārī (9/15), Fatḥ al-Bārī of Ibn Ḥajar (12/270)

(2) Ḥilyat al-Awliyāʾ of Abū Nuʿaym al-Aṣbahānī (8/253)

(3) Al-Kifāya Fī Maʿrifat Uṣūl ʿIlm al-Riwāya of al-Khaṭīb al-Baghdādī (2/171-172)

(4) Imām al-Ḏahabī said, "By Allah the Great, ʿAlī uttered this, and it is mass-transmitted (*mutawātir*) from him. That is because he uttered it whilst on Kufa's pulpit. So may Allah damn the Rāfiḍa, how ignorant are they!" See Tārīkh al-Islam of al-Ḏahabī (2/68).

بَلْ كُلُّ شِيعَتِهِ الَّذِينَ قَاتَلُوا مَعَهُ عَدُوَّهُ كَانُوا مَعَ سَائِرِ الْمُسْلِمِينَ يُقَدِّمُونَ أَبَا بَكْرٍ وَعُمَرَ؛ إِلَّا مَنْ كَانَ عَلِيٌّ يُنْكِرُ عَلَيْهِ وَيَذُمُّهُ مَعَ قِلَّتِهِمْ فِي عَهْدِ عَلِيٍّ وَخُمُولِهِمْ.

كَانُوا ثَلَاثَ طَوَائِفَ: طَائِفَةٌ غَلَتْ فِيهِ كَالَّتِي ادَّعَتْ فِيهِ الْإِلَهِيَّةَ، وَهَؤُلَاءِ حَرَّقَهُمْ عَلِيٌّ بِالنَّارِ. وَطَائِفَةٌ كَانَتْ تَسُبُّ أَبَا بَكْرٍ، وَكَانَ رَأْسُهُمْ عَبْدَ اللَّهِ بْنَ سَبَأٍ، فَلَمَّا بَلَغَ عَلِيًّا ذَلِكَ طَلَبَ قَتْلَهُ فَهَرَبَ مِنْهُ. وَطَائِفَةٌ كَانَتْ تُفَضِّلُهُ عَلَى أَبِي بَكْرٍ وَعُمَرَ، قَالَ: "لَا يَبْلُغُنِي عَنْ أَحَدٍ مِنْكُمْ أَنَّهُ فَضَّلَنِي عَلَى أَبِي بَكْرٍ وَعُمَرَ إِلَّا جَلَدْته حَدَّ الْمُفْتَرِي."

وَقَدْ رُوِيَ عَنْ عَلِيٍّ مِنْ نَحْوِ ثَمَانِينَ وَجْهًا وَأَكْثَرَ أَنَّهُ قَالَ عَلَى مِنْبَرِ الْكُوفَةِ: "خَيْرُ هَذِهِ الْأُمَّةِ بَعْدَ نَبِيِّهَا أَبُو بَكْرٍ وَعُمَرُ."

This has also been established in *Ṣaḥīḥ al-Bukhārī* and other sources through the specific transmission of men from the tribe of Hamadān – about whom ʿAlī had said, "If I were a gatekeeper at the gate of Heaven, I would have said to Hamdān, 'Enter with peace!'"(1) It was transmitted by Sufyān al-Thawrī through Munḏir al-Thawrī, and both were from Hamdān.

Al-Bukhārī reported it from Muḥummad ibn Kathīr, he said: Sufyān al-Thawrī informed us, Jāmiʿ ibn Shaddād informed us, Abū Yaʿlā Munḏir al-Thawrī informed us, from Muḥammad ibn al-Ḥanafiyya, he said, "I once said to my father, 'Father, who are the best of people after the Messenger of Allah ﷺ?' He replied, 'Son, do you not know?' I said, 'No.' He said, 'Abū Bakr.' I said, 'Then who?' He said, 'Then ʿUmar.'"(2)

ʿAlī had said this to his own son – with whom he did not practice *taqiyya* – and to his intimate companions. ʿAlī used to punish those who ranked him above Abū Bakr and ʿUmar. It is impermissible for a person acting out of humility to punish all those who utter the truth and to label them as slanderers.(3)

The pinnacle of all merits is knowledge. Anyone who is superior to prophets, *ṣaḥāba*, and others is thus more knowledgeable than them. Allah said, "Are those who know and those who do not know equal? [Quran 39:9]" The evidences for this are plentiful, and the scholars' statements in its regard are numerous.

---

(1) Al-Tārīkh al-Kabīr of Ibn Abī Khaythama – al-Sifr al-Thālith (3/172). There is a discontinuity in this isnād; however, Ibn Taymiyya's appeal to this report is tangential. He merely sited it to emphacize that the aforementioned tradition's transmitters were from a Kufan tribe beloved to and closely aligned with ʿAlī.

It should be noted that Sufyān al-Thawrī was from Thawr Ṭābikha, not Hamdān. See Tārīkh al-Islām of al-Ḏahabī (4/382). Nonetheless, his point is valid with respect to Munḏir al-Thawrī, who was not only from the Kufan tribe of Hamdān, but also closely aligned with *Ahlulbayt*.

(2) Ṣaḥīḥ al-Bukhārī (5/7)

(3) This is a preemptive rebuttal to Shi'ites who may retort in an *ad hoc* fashion

وَقَدْ ثَبَتَ فِي صَحِيحِ الْبُخَارِيِّ وَغَيْرِهِ مِنْ رِوَايَةِ رِجَالِ همدان خَاصَّةً – الَّتِي يَقُولُ فِيهَا عَلِيٌّ: وَلَوْ كُنْت بَوَّابًا عَلَى بَابِ جَنَّةٍ لَقُلْت لهمدان أُدْخُلِي بِسَلَامِ – مِنْ رِوَايَةِ سُفْيَانَ الثَّوْرِيِّ، عَنْ مُنْذِرٍ الثَّوْرِيِّ، وَكِلَاهُمَا مِنْ همدان.

رَوَاهُ الْبُخَارِيُّ عَنْ مُحَمَّدِ بْنِ كَثِيرٍ، قَالَ: حَدَّثَنَا سُفْيَانُ الثَّوْرِيُّ، حَدَّثَنَا: جَامِعُ بْنُ شَدَّادٍ، حَدَّثَنَا: أَبُو يَعْلَى مُنْذِرٌ الثَّوْرِيُّ، عَنْ مُحَمَّدِ بْنِ الْحَنَفِيَّةِ، قَالَ: قُلْت لِأَبِي: "يَا أَبَتِ مَنْ خَيْرُ النَّاسِ بَعْدَ رَسُولِ اللَّهِ ﷺ؟" فَقَالَ: "يَا بُنَيَّ، أَوَمَا تَعْرِفُ؟" فَقُلْت: "لَا." فَقَالَ: "أَبُو بَكْرٍ." قُلْت: "ثُمَّ مَنْ؟" قَالَ: "ثُمَّ عُمَرُ."

وَهَذَا يَقُولُهُ لِابْنِهِ الَّذِي لَا يَتَّقِيه وَلِخَاصَّتِهِ، وَيَتَقَدَّمُ بِعُقُوبَةِ مَنْ يُفَضِّلُهُ عَلَيْهِمَا. وَالْمُتَوَاضِعُ لَا يَجُوزُ لَهُ أَنْ يَتَقَدَّمَ بِعُقُوبَةِ كُلِّ مَنْ قَالَ الْحَقَّ وَلَا يَجُوزُ أَنْ يُسَمِّيَهُ مُفْتَرِيًا.

وَرَأْسُ الْفَضَائِلِ الْعِلْمُ، وَكُلُّ مَنْ كَانَ أَفْضَلَ مَنْ غَيْرِهِ مِنْ الْأَنْبِيَاءِ وَالصَّحَابَةِ وَغَيْرِهِمْ فَإِنَّهُ أَعْلَمُ مِنْهُ. قَالَ تَعَالَى: {هَلْ يَسْتَوِي الَّذِينَ يَعْلَمُونَ وَالَّذِينَ لَا يَعْلَمُونَ}. وَالدَّلَائِلُ عَلَى ذَلِكَ كَثِيرَةٌ وَكَلَامُ الْعُلَمَاءِ فِي ذَلِكَ كَثِيرٌ.

---

by arguing that ʿAlī was practicing *taqiyya* when he made this declaration. Of course, such a notion is quite preposterous when considering that ʿAlī had uttered this statement to his own son. Its preposterousness is further pronounced when one considers that it was likely uttered during ʿAlī's reign as caliph at the height of his power and authority.

Ibn Taymiyya also addresses another *ad hoc* retort, which is the claim that ʿAlī uttered such statements out of humility, implying that they bear no significance beyond that. One issue with this appeal, among many, is that it would be morally reprehensible for ʿAlī in this case to punish those who ranked him above Abū Bakr and ʿUmar and label them as slanderers. Ultimately, such Twelver *ad hoc* appeals presuppose a Twelver reading of history when engaging with these authentic traditions in this manner, and they are hence not posited in good faith.

Regarding the Prophet's ﷺ statement, "The most judicious of you is ʿAlī," it has not been reported through an authentic or weak isnād by any of the authors of the Six Books (*al-Kutub al-Sitta*) or the renowned *Musnads,* not Aḥmed [ibn Ḥanbal] or anyone else. Rather, it is only reported through those known for forgery. ʿUmar ibn al-Khaṭṭāb, however, did say, "Ubay is the most recightful among us, and ʿAlī is the most judicious among us."(1) He uttered this after Abū Bakr's death.

The tradition in al-Tirmiḏī and other sources where the Prophet ﷺ said, "The most knowledgeable of my *Ummah* in *ḥalāl* and *ḥarām* is Muʿāḏ ibn Jabal, and the most knowledgeable in inheritance is Zayd ibn Thābit," has no mention of ʿAlī.(2) The variant that mentions ʿAlī, despite its weakness, mentions that Muʿāḏ ibn Jabal is the most knowledgeable in *ḥalāl* and *ḥarām* and that Zayd ibn Thābit is the most knowledgeable in inheritance.(3)

Assuming this ḥadīth is authentic, the individual most knowledgeable in *ḥalāl* and *ḥarām* [mentioned therein] would be more knowledgeable than the individual most knowledgeable in adjudication. That is because one who specializes in adjudication merely resolves disputes based on apparent evidence, though it is possible that underlying truth is contrary to it. As the Prophet ﷺ said, "You bring your disputes to me, and perhaps some of you may be more convincingly articulate with their arguments than others. I merely rule based on what I hear. If I grant anyone something that rightfully belongs to his brother, then he should not take it, for I merely would be granting him a piece of the Hellfire."(4)

---

(1) Ṣaḥīḥ al-Bukhārī (6/19)

(2) Al-Jāmiʿ al-Kabīr of al-Tirmiḏī (6/127)

(3) The ḥadīth scholar, Ibn ʿAbdilHādī, analyzed this tradition in depth in a treatise of his, highlighting its defects. See Majmūʿ Rasāʾil al-Ḥāfiẓ Ibn ʿAbdilHādī (p. 51-81).

(4) Ṣaḥīḥ al-Bukhārī (3/180), Ṣaḥīḥ Muslim (3/1337)

وَأَمَّا قَوْلُهُ: {أَقْضَاكُمْ عَلِيٌّ}، فَلَمْ يَرْوِهِ أَحَدٌ مِنْ أَهْلِ الْكُتُبِ السِّتَّةِ وَلَا أَهْلُ الْمَسَانِيدِ الْمَشْهُورَةِ لَا أَحْمَدُ وَلَا غَيْرُهُ بِإِسْنَادٍ صَحِيحٍ وَلَا ضَعِيفٍ. وَإِنَّمَا يُرْوَى مِنْ طَرِيقِ مَنْ هُوَ مَعْرُوفٌ بِالْكَذِبِ. وَلَكِنْ قَالَ عُمَرُ بْنُ الْخَطَّابِ: "أَبِي أَقْرَؤُنَا، وَعَلِيٌّ أَقْضَانَا." وَهَذَا قَالَهُ بَعْدَ مَوْتِ أَبِي بَكْرٍ.

وَالَّذِي فِي التِّرْمِذِيِّ وَغَيْرِهِ أَنَّ النَّبِيَّ ﷺ قَالَ: {أَعْلَمُ أُمَّتِي بِالْحَلَالِ وَالْحَرَامِ مُعَاذُ بْنُ جَبَلٍ وَأَعْلَمُهَا بِالْفَرَائِضِ زَيْدُ بْنُ ثَابِتٍ}، وَلَيْسَ فِيهِ ذِكْرَ عَلِيٍّ. وَالْحَدِيثُ الَّذِي فِيهِ ذِكْرَ عَلِيٍّ – مَعَ ضَعْفِهِ – فِيهِ أَنَّ مُعَاذَ بْنَ جَبَلٍ أَعْلَمُ بِالْحَلَالِ وَالْحَرَامِ وَزَيْدَ بْنَ ثَابِتٍ أَعْلَمُ بِالْفَرَائِضِ.

فَلَوْ قُدِّرَ صِحَّةُ هَذَا الْحَدِيثِ لَكَانَ الْأَعْلَمُ بِالْحَلَالِ وَالْحَرَامِ أَوْسَعُ عِلْمًا مِنْ الْأَعْلَمِ بِالْقَضَاءِ، لِأَنَّ الَّذِي يَخْتَصُّ بِالْقَضَاءِ إِنَّمَا هُوَ فَصل الْخُصُومَاتِ فِي الظَّاهِرِ مَعَ جَوَازِ أَنْ يَكُونَ الْبَاطِنُ بِخِلَافِهِ. كَمَا قَالَ النَّبِيُّ ﷺ: {إِنَّكُمْ تَخْتَصِمُونَ إِلَيَّ، وَلَعَلَّ بَعْضَكُمْ أَنْ يَكُونَ أَلْحَن بِحُجَّتِهِ مِنْ بَعْضٍ. وَإِنَّمَا أَقْضِي بِنَحْوِ مَا أَسْمَعُ، فَمَنْ قَضَيْت لَهُ مِنْ حَقِّ أَخِيهِ شَيْئًا فَلَا يَأْخُذْهُ، فَإِنَّمَا أَقْطَعُ لَهُ قِطْعَةً مِنْ النَّارِ}.

The Master of all judges ﷺ has mentioned that his adjudication does not make the *ḥarām* permissible. Rather, it is impermissible for a Muslim to accept anything granted to him by the Prophet's ﷺ judgement when it actually belongs to another person. Knowledge in the *ḥalāl* and the *ḥarām*, however, encompasses both the apparent and the concealed, so the one more knowledgeable in it is more knowledgeable in the faith as a whole.

Furthermore, adjudication is of two types. One is when both parties are in mutual denial, such as when one party claims something, and the other impugnes it. The judge thus adjucates between them based on evidence and such. The second type is when both parties are not in mutual denial: they validate each other, but they do not know the specifities of their entitlements. An example would be a dispute over the distribution of inheritance, or mutual obligations between spouses, or the respective rights of business partners, and similar things. This subject falls under the umbrella of *ḥalāl* and *ḥarām*. Consequently, if a mutually trusted individual issues them a verdict, then he would have sufficed them, negating the need of an adjudicator between them. Rather, an adjudicator is only needed during mutual denial, and such scenarios mostly result from depravity. They may also arise from forgetfulness.

As for *ḥalāl* and *ḥarām*, it is needed by every person, righteous and depraved alike. As for matters confined to adjudication, only a small amount of the pious are in need of it. For this reason, when Abū Bakr instructed ʿUmar to adjudicate between the people, one year elapsed without any two parties presenting their disputes to him.[1] If the Prophet's ﷺ verdicts of this nature were quantified, they would not amount to ten verdicts. How could that compare to the Prophet's ﷺ speech regarding *ḥalāl* and *ḥarām*, which is the foundation of Islam needed by the scholars and the laity alike?

---

(1) Akhbār al-Quḍāt of al-Ḍabbī (1/104), Kitāb al-Ṭabaqāt al-Kabīr (3/168)

فَقَدْ أَخْبَرَ سَيِّدُ الْقُضَاةِ ﷺ أَنَّ قَضَاءَهُ لَا يُحِلُّ الْحَرَامَ، بَلْ يَحْرُمُ عَلَى الْمُسْلِمِ أَنْ يَأْخُذَ بِقَضَائِهِ مَا قَضَى لَهُ بِهِ مِنْ حَقِّ الْغَيْرِ. وَعِلْمُ الْحَلَالِ وَالْحَرَامِ يَتَنَاوَلُ الظَّاهِرَ وَالْبَاطِنَ، فَكَانَ الْأَعْلَمُ بِهِ أَعْلَمَ بِالدِّينِ.

وَأَيْضًا فَالْقَضَاءُ نَوْعَانِ: أَحَدُهُمَا الْحُكْمُ عِنْدَ تَجَاحُدِ الْخَصْمَيْنِ، مِثْلُ أَنْ يَدَّعِيَ أَحَدُهُمَا أَمْرًا يُكَذِّبُهُ الْآخَرُ فِيهِ فَيَحْكُمُ فِيهِ بِالْبَيِّنَةِ وَنَحْوِهَا. وَالثَّانِي مَا لَا يَتَجَاحَدَانِ فِيهِ –يَتَصَادَقَانِ– وَلَكِنْ لَا يَعْلَمَانِ مَا يَسْتَحِقُّ كُلٌّ مِنْهُمَا، كَتَنَازُعِهِمَا فِي قَسْمِ فَرِيضَةٍ أَوْ فِيمَا يَجِبُ لِكُلٍّ مِنَ الزَّوْجَيْنِ عَلَى الْآخَرِ أَوْ فِيمَا يَسْتَحِقُّهُ كُلٌّ مِنَ الشَّرِيكَيْنِ وَنَحْوِ ذَلِكَ؛ فَهَذَا الْبَابُ هُوَ مِنْ أَبْوَابِ الْحَلَالِ وَالْحَرَامِ. فَإِذَا أَفْتَاهُمَا مَنْ يَرْضَيَانِ بِقَوْلِهِ كَفَاهُمَا ذَلِكَ وَلَمْ يَحْتَاجَا إِلَى مَنْ يَحْكُمُ بَيْنَهُمَا. وَإِنَّمَا يَحْتَاجَانِ إِلَى حَاكِمٍ عِنْدَ التَّجَاحُدِ، وَذَاكَ إِنَّمَا يَكُونُ فِي الْأَغْلَبِ مَعَ الْفُجُورِ، وَقَدْ يَكُونُ مَعَ النِّسْيَانِ.

فَأَمَّا الْحَلَالُ وَالْحَرَامُ فَيَحْتَاجُ إِلَيْهِ كُلُّ أَحَدٍ مِنْ بَرٍّ وَفَاجِرٍ، وَمَا يَخْتَصُّ بِالْقَضَاءِ لَا يَحْتَاجُ إِلَيْهِ إِلَّا قَلِيلٌ مِنَ الْأَبْرَارِ. وَلِهَذَا لَمَّا أَمَرَ أَبُو بَكْرٍ عُمَرَ أَنْ يَقْضِيَ بَيْنَ النَّاسِ مَكَثَ حَوْلًا لَمْ يَتَحَاكَمْ اثْنَانِ فِي شَيْءٍ. وَلَوْ عَدَّ مَجْمُوعَ مَا قَضَى النَّبِيُّ ﷺ مِنْ هَذَا النَّوْعِ لَمْ يَبْلُغْ عَشَرَ حُكُومَاتٍ. فَأَيْنَ هَذَا مِنْ كَلَامِهِ فِي الْحَلَالِ وَالْحَرَامِ الَّذِي هُوَ قِوَامُ دِينِ الْإِسْلَامِ يَحْتَاجُ إِلَيْهِ الْخَاصُّ وَالْعَامُّ؟

His statement, "The most knowledgeable of them in *ḥalāl* and *ḥarām* is Muʿāḏ ibn Jabal," is more authentic than his statement, "The most judicious among you is ʿAlī," per agreement of the scholars of ḥadīth, assuming the tradition is reliable.(1) If it is stronger in isnād and more explicit in indication, then it should be evident that anyone who cites it to argue for ʿAlī's superiority to Muʿāḏ ibn Jabal in knowledge is ignorant. Moreover, how would it then be [if the ḥadīth were cited to argue for ʿAlī's superiority in knowledge] to Abū Bakr and ʿUmar, who are both superior to Muʿāḏ ibn Jabal in knowledege?! This is considering the fact that the ḥadīth mentioning Muʿāḏ and Zayd is weakened by some and declared *ḥasan* by some, while the ḥadīth mentioning ʿAlī is weak.

As for the ḥadīth, "I am the city of knowledge," it is even weaker and frailer. For this reason, it is counted among the forged fabrications, even though al-Tirmiḏī reported it.(2) Ibn al-Jawzī consequently mentioned it in the Fabrications (*al-Mawḍūʿāt*), and he demonstrated its fabrication through all of its routes.(3)

Falsehood is recognized in its contents (*matn*): its isnād is not even in need of inspection. Had the Prophet ﷺ been the city of knowledge, having only one gate, it would be improper for just one individual to be the conveyor from him.

---

(1) This tradition, in its final and longest form, exhibited several interpolations, which is why Ibn Taymiyya emphasizes that some clauses therein are more authentic than others. See al-Faṣl li-l-Waṣl al-Mudraj Fī al-Naql of al-Khaṭīb al-Baghdādī (p. 676-687).

(2) Lest anyone misconstrue al-Tirmiḏī's transmission of this ḥadīth as an endorsement of its contents, it should be noted that al-Tirmiḏī himself condemned the tradition upon mentioning it in his book. Al-Tirmiḏī commented immediately after it, saying, "This ḥadīth is *gharīb* and disapproved (*munkar*)...." See al-Jāmiʿ al-Kabīr of al-Tirmiḏī (6/85-86).

(3) Kitāb al-Mawḍūʿāt al-Kubrā of Ibn al-Jawzī (1/349-355). The master of ḥadīth, al-ʿUqaylī, also commented on this tradition, saying, "Not a single ḥadīth associated with this *matn* is authentic." See Kitāb al-Ḍuʿafāʾ al-Kabīr of al-ʿUqaylī (3/150). Many scholars similarly disparaged this tradition, and what was listed here should be sufficient in this context.

وَقَوْلُهُ: {أَعْلَمُهُمْ بِالْحَلَالِ وَالْحَرَامِ مُعَاذُ بْنُ جَبَلٍ} أَقْرَبُ إِلَى الصِّحَّةِ بِاتِّفَاقِ عُلَمَاءِ الْحَدِيثِ مِنْ قَوْلِهِ {أَقْضَاكُمْ عَلِيٌّ} لَوْ كَانَ مِمَّا يُحْتَجُّ بِهِ. وَإِذَا كَانَ ذَلِكَ أَصَحَّ إِسْنَادًا وَأَظْهَرَ دَلَالَةً عُلِمَ أَنَّ الْمُحْتَجَّ بِذَلِكَ عَلَى أَنَّ عَلِيًّا أَعْلَمُ مِنْ مُعَاذِ بْنِ جَبَلٍ جَاهِلٌ، فَكَيْفَ مِنْ أَبِي بَكْرٍ وَعُمَرَ اللَّذَيْنِ هُمَا أَعْلَمُ مِنْ مُعَاذِ بْنِ جَبَلٍ؟! مَعَ أَنَّ الْحَدِيثَ الَّذِي فِيهِ ذِكْرُ مُعَاذٍ وَزَيْدٍ يُضَعِّفُهُ بَعْضُهُمْ وَيُحَسِّنُهُ بَعْضُهُمْ، وَأَمَّا الْحَدِيثُ الَّذِي فِيهِ ذِكْرُ عَلِيٍّ فَإِنَّهُ ضَعِيفٌ.

وَأَمَّا حَدِيثُ {أَنَا مَدِينَةُ الْعِلْمِ} فَأَضْعَفُ وَأَوْهَى، وَلِهَذَا إِنَّمَا يُعَدُّ فِي الْمَوْضُوعَاتِ الْمَكْذُوبَاتِ، وَإِنْ كَانَ التِّرْمِذِيُّ قَدْ رَوَاهُ. وَلِهَذَا ذَكَرَهُ ابْنُ الْجَوْزِيِّ فِي «الْمَوْضُوعَاتِ» وَبَيَّنَ أَنَّهُ مَوْضُوعٌ مِنْ سَائِرِ طُرُقِهِ.

وَالْكَذِبُ يُعْرَفُ مِنْ نَفْسِ مَتْنِهِ لَا يَحْتَاجُ إِلَى النَّظَرِ فِي إِسْنَادِهِ. فَإِنَّ النَّبِيَّ ﷺ إِذَا كَانَ {مَدِينَةَ الْعِلْمِ} لَمْ يَكُنْ لِهَذِهِ الْمَدِينَةِ إِلَّا بَابٌ وَاحِدٌ، وَلَا يَجُوزُ أَنْ يَكُونَ الْمُبَلِّغُ عَنْهُ وَاحِدًا.

Rather, the conveyor from the Prophet ﷺ must be the people of mass-transmission (*tawātur*) whose transmission yields definitive knowledge for the absent. Transmission from a single individual does not yield definitive knowledge, unless it is supported by indicators. Those indicators are either absent or inconspicuous to many or most people, which would bar them from yielding definitive knowledge from the Quran and the *Sunnah* that actually are mass-transmitted (*mutawātira*). In contrast, mass-transmitted (*mutawātir*) transmission yields definitive knowledge for the scholars and the laity alike.

This ḥadīth was merely fabricated by a heretic (*zindīq*) or an ignoramus who misconstrued it as praise. It is the heretics' stepping stone towards discrediting all knowledge of the faith, as it was purportedly conveyed by only one of the *Ṣaḥāba*. Furthermore, this [ḥadīth] is contrary to what is known by mass-transmission (*tawātur*). All Muslim cities have received knowledge from the Messenger of Allah ﷺ through other than ʿAlī. As for the people of Medīna and Mecca, their case is apparent. Similar to that are the people of al-Shām and al-Baṣra, for they used to sparsely transmit from ʿAlī. Most of his knowledge was with the people of Kufa, yet they, nonetheless, had already learned the Quran and Sunnah prior to ʿUthmān's reign, let alone ʿAlī's caliphate.(1)

The most understanding and knowledgeable from the people of Medīna had learned the religion during ʿUmar's caliphate. Prior to that, none of them learned anything from ʿAlī except those who had learned from him while he was in Yemen as they simultaneously learned from Muʿāḏ ibn Jabal.

---

(1) That is because ʿUmar ibn al-Khaṭṭāb (Allah be pleased with him) had dispatched ʿAbdullāh ibn Masʿūd to the city of Kufa during his reign to educate its inhabitants and teach them the Quran . Ibn Masʿūd's blessed knowledge spread across the city, ultimately giving rise to schools and scholars who were inspired and influenced by his legacy. This occurred prior to ʿAlī's arrival to the city of Kufa. See al-Mustadrak of al-Ḥākim (6/184).

بَلْ يَجِبُ أَنْ يَكُونَ الْمُبَلِّغُ عَنْهُ أَهْلَ التَّوَاتُرِ الَّذِينَ يَحْصُلُ الْعِلْمُ بِخَبَرِهِمْ لِلْغَائِبِ وَرِوَايَةُ الْوَاحِدِ لَا تُفِيدُ الْعِلْمَ إِلَّا مَعَ قَرَائِنَ. وَتِلْكَ الْقَرَائِنُ إِمَّا أَنْ تَكُونَ مُنْتَفِيَةً وَإِمَّا أَنْ تَكُونَ خَفِيَّةً عَنْ كَثِيرٍ مِنَ النَّاسِ أَوْ أَكْثَرِهِمْ، فَلَا يَحْصُلُ لَهُمْ الْعِلْمُ بِالْقُرْآنِ وَالسُّنَّةِ الْمُتَوَاتِرَةِ؛ بِخِلَافِ النَّقْلِ الْمُتَوَاتِرِ: الَّذِي يَحْصُلُ بِهِ الْعِلْمُ لِلْخَاصِّ وَالْعَامِّ.

وَهَذَا الْحَدِيثُ إِنَّمَا افْتَرَاهُ زِنْدِيقٌ أَوْ جَاهِلٌ ظَنَّهُ مَدْحًا، وَهُوَ مُطَرِّقُ الزَّنَادِقَةِ إِلَى الْقَدْحِ فِي عِلْمِ الدِّينِ إِذْ لَمْ يُبَلِّغْهُ إِلَّا وَاحِدٌ مِنَ الصَّحَابَةِ. ثُمَّ إِنَّ هَذَا خِلَافُ الْمَعْلُومِ بِالتَّوَاتُرِ. فَإِنَّ جَمِيعَ مَدَائِنِ الْمُسْلِمِينَ بَلَغَهُمْ الْعِلْمُ عَنْ رَسُولِ اللَّهِ ﷺ مِنْ غَيْرِ طَرِيقِ عَلِيٍّ رَضِيَ اللَّهُ عَنْهُ. أَمَّا أَهْلُ الْمَدِينَةِ وَمَكَّةَ فَالْأَمْرُ فِيهِمْ ظَاهِرٌ، وَكَذَلِكَ أَهْلُ الشَّامِ وَالْبَصْرَةِ، فَإِنَّ هَؤُلَاءِ لَمْ يَكُونُوا يَرْوُونَ عَنْ عَلِيٍّ إِلَّا شَيْئًا قَلِيلًا. وَإِنَّمَا غَالِبُ عِلْمِهِ كَانَ فِي أَهْلِ الْكُوفَةِ، وَمَعَ هَذَا فَقَدْ كَانُوا تَعَلَّمُوا الْقُرْآنَ وَالسُّنَّةَ قَبْلَ أَنْ يَتَوَلَّى عُثْمَانُ، فَضْلًا عَنْ خِلَافَةِ عَلِيٍّ.

وَكَانَ أَفْقَهَ أَهْلِ الْمَدِينَةِ وَأَعْلَمَهُمْ تَعَلَّمُوا الدِّينَ فِي خِلَافَةِ عُمَرَ، وَقَبْلَ ذَلِكَ لَمْ يَتَعَلَّمْ أَحَدٌ مِنْهُمْ مِنْ عَلِيٍّ شَيْئًا إِلَّا مَنْ تَعَلَّمَ مِنْهُ لَمَّا كَانَ بِالْيَمَنِ كَمَا تَعَلَّمُوا حِينَئِذٍ مِنْ مُعَاذِ بْنِ جَبَلٍ.

Muʿāḏ ibn Jabal's residence and tutelage among the people of Yemen was greater than ʿAlī's residence and tutelage therein. Consequently, the people of Yemen transmitted more from Muʿāḏ than they did from ʿAlī. Shurayḥ and other senior tābiʿīn learned *Fiqh* from Muʿāḏ. By the time ʿAlī arrived to Kufa, Shurayḥ had already presided as a judge in the city. ʿAlī, during his caliphate, entrusted the judiciary to Shurayḥ and ʿAbīda al-Salmānī, and both had learned Fiqh from other than him.

Knowledge of Islam had spread in the cities of Islam – Hejaz, al-Shām, Yemen, Iraq, Khurāsān, Egypt, al-Maghrib – prior to ʿAlī's arrival to Kufa. When he arrived to Kufa, most of the knowledge that he disseminated was also disseminated by other *Ṣaḥāba*. For every bit of knowledge exclusively conveyed by ʿAlī, there are others who exclusively conveyed even more knowledge.

The broad dissemination [of knowledge] through rulership that occurred with Abū Bakr, ʿUmar, and ʿUthmān is greater than that of ʿAlī. As for specialized dissemination, Ibn ʿAbbās was more prolific than ʿAlī in *fatwā*, and Abū Hurayra was more prolific than him in transmission. ʿAlī, however, was more knowledgeable than them both, similar to how Abū Bakr and ʿUmar were more knowledgeable than both as well. The Rightly Guided Caliphs partook in the dissemination of broad knowledge, which was more needed by the people than the specialized knowledge disseminated by its associates.

As for what the people of deceit and ignorance report about ʿAlī's possession of exclusive knowledge that the *Ṣaḥāba* lacked, it is all dubious. It has been established from ʿAlī in the *Ṣaḥīḥ* that it was once said to him, "Do you possess anything [special] from the Messenger of Allah ﷺ?" ʿAlī replied, "No. By the One who split the seed and created the soul, I possess nothing but the understanding of Allah's book that He grants to a slave, and what is in this parchment."

وَكَانَ مُقَامُ مُعَاذِ بْنِ جَبَلٍ فِي أَهْلِ الْيَمَنِ وَتَعْلِيمُهُ لَهُمْ أَكْثَرَ مِنْ مَقَامِ عَلِيٍّ وَتَعْلِيمِهِ. وَلِهَذَا رَوَى أَهْلُ الْيَمَنِ عَنْ مُعَاذٍ أَكْثَرَ مِمَّا رَوَوْهُ عَنْ عَلِيٍّ. وشريح وَغَيْرِهِ مَنْ أَكَابِرِ التَّابِعِينَ إِنَّمَا تَفقَّهُوا عَلَى مُعَاذٍ، وَلَمَّا قَدِمَ عَلِيٌّ الْكُوفَةَ كَانَ شريح قَاضِيًا فِيهَا قَبْلَ ذَلِكَ. وَعَلِيٌّ وَجَدَ عَلَى الْقَضَاءِ فِي خِلَافَتِهِ شريحا وعَبِيدة السلماني، وَكِلَاهُمَا تَفَقَّهَ عَلَى غَيْرِهِ.

فَإِذا كَانَ عِلْمُ الْإِسْلَامِ انْتَشَرَ فِي مَدَائِنِ الْإِسْلَامِ بِالْحِجَازِ وَالشَّامِ وَالْيَمَنِ وَالْعِرَاقِ وَخُرَاسَانَ وَمِصْرَ وَالْمَغْرِبِ قَبْلَ أَنْ يَقْدُمَ إِلَى الْكُوفَةِ، وَلَمَّا صَارَ إِلَى الْكُوفَةِ عَامَّةُ مَا بَلَغَهُ مِنَ الْعِلْمِ بَلَّغَهُ غَيْرُهُ مِنَ الصَّحَابَةِ، وَلَمْ يَخْتَصَّ عَلِيٌّ بِتَبْلِيغِ شَيْءٍ مِنَ الْعِلْمِ إِلَّا وَقَدْ اخْتَصَّ غَيْرُهُ بِمَا هُوَ أَكْثَرُ مِنْهُ.

فَالتَّبْلِيغُ الْعَامُّ الْحَاصِلُ بِالْوِلَايَةِ حَصَلَ لِأَبِي بَكْرٍ وَعُمَرَ وَعُثْمَانَ مِنْهُ أَكْثَرُ مِمَّا حَصَلَ لِعَلِيٍّ. وَأَمَّا الْخَاصُّ فَابْنُ عَبَّاسٍ كَانَ أَكْثَرَ فُتْيَا مِنْهُ وَأَبُو هُرَيْرَةَ أَكْثَرَ رِوَايَةً مِنْهُ، وَعَلِيٌّ أَعْلَمُ مِنْهُمَا، كَمَا أَنَّ أَبَا بَكْرٍ وَعُمَرَ وَعُثْمَانَ أَعْلَمُ مِنْهُمَا أَيْضًا. فَإِنَّ الْخُلَفَاءَ الرَّاشِدِينَ قَامُوا مِنْ تَبْلِيغِ الْعِلْمِ الْعَامِّ بِمَا كَانَ النَّاسُ أَحْوَجَ إِلَيْهِ مِمَّا بَلَّغَهُ مَنْ بَلَّغَ بَعْضَ الْعِلْمِ الْخَاصِّ.

وَأَمَّا مَا يَرْوِيه أَهْلُ الْكَذِبِ وَالْجَهْلِ مِنْ اخْتِصَاصِ عَلِيٍّ بِعِلْمٍ انْفَرَدَ بِهِ عَنِ الصَّحَابَةِ فَكُلُّهُ بَاطِلٌ، وَقَدْ ثَبَتَ عَنْهُ فِي الصَّحِيحِ أَنَّهُ قِيلَ لَهُ: {هَلْ عِنْدَكُمْ مِنْ رَسُولِ اللَّهِ ﷺ شَيْءٌ؟ فَقَالَ: لَا وَالَّذِي فَلَقَ الْحَبَّةَ وَبَرَأَ النَّسَمَةَ إِلَّا فَهْمًا يُؤْتِيهِ اللَّهُ عَبْدًا فِي كِتَابِهِ وَمَا فِي هَذِهِ الصَّحِيفَةِ}.

That parchment contained the ages of camels for which blood money is due. It also contained guidelines on the ransom of prisoners and the ordinance that a Muslim should not be executed in retribution for killing a disbeliever.(1)

In one variant, ʿAlī was asked, "Did the Messenger of Allah entrust you with anything that he did not share with the people?" and ʿAlī denied that.(2)

There are other ḥadīths demonstrating that anyone who claims the Prophet ﷺ had endowed ʿAlī with exclusive knowledge is lying about the Prophet ﷺ. What is claimed by some of the ignoramuses regarding ʿAlī drinking from the water used to wash the Prophet's ﷺ corpse, thereby inheriting all knowledge of the first and the last [generations] is among the most hideous of brazen of lies. Drinking the water used to cleanse a dead person's body is impermissible, and ʿAlī did not drink any of that. (3) If this entails knowledge, then all of those present during the washing would have shared it with him. This was not reported by anyone from the people of knowledge.

Likewise is what is claimed about ʿAlī possessing esoteric (*bāṭin*) knowledge that distinguished him from Abū Bakr, ʿUmar, and others. This is from the beliefs held by the heretical esoteresists (*al-Malāḥida al-Bāṭiniyya*) and their likes who are even more disbelieving than them (the Rāfiḍa).

---

(1) Ṣaḥīḥ al-Bukhārī (1/33, 4/69, 9/11-12)

(2) Musnad Aḥmed ibn Ḥanbal (2/286)

(3) The idea that ʿAlī drank the water used to wash the Messenger of Allah's body was reported from Jaʿfar al-Ṣādiq via a mediocre isnād, and its ascription to him is in need of further verification. Additionally, Jaʿfar's transmission of the account is disconnected, as he is at least two generations removed from the purported incident. Nonetheless, his report contains no reference to the notion that ʿAlī inherited all knowledge by drinking this water, a blatantly fallacious Shi'ite accretion. See Musnad Aḥmed ibn Ḥanbal (4/229).

وَكَانَ فِيهَا عُقُولُ الدِّيَاتِ – أَيْ: أَسْنَانُ الْإِبِلِ الَّتِي تَجِبُ فِيهِ الدِّيَةُ – وَفِيهَا فِكَاكُ الْأَسِيرِ وَفِيهَا لَا يُقْتَلُ مُسْلِمٌ بِكَافِرٍ.

وَفِي لَفْظٍ: "هَلْ عَهِدَ إِلَيْكُمْ رَسُولُ اللَّهِ ﷺ شَيْئًا لَمْ يَعْهَدْهُ إِلَى النَّاسِ؟" فَنَفَى ذَلِكَ.

إِلَى غَيْرِ ذَلِكَ مِنَ الْأَحَادِيثِ عَنْهُ الَّتِي تَدُلُّ عَلَى أَنَّ كُلَّ مَنْ ادَّعَى أَنَّ النَّبِيَّ ﷺ خَصَّهُ بِعِلْمٍ فَقَدْ كَذَبَ عَلَيْهِ. وَمَا يَقُولُهُ بَعْضُ الْجُهَّالِ أَنَّهُ شَرِبَ مِنْ غُسْلِ النَّبِيِّ ﷺ فَأَوْرَثَهُ عِلْمَ الْأَوَّلِينَ والآخرين مِنْ أَقْبَحِ الْكَذِبِ الْبَارِدِ، فَإِنَّ شُرْبَ غُسْلِ الْمَيِّتِ لَيْسَ بِمَشْرُوعٍ وَلَا شَرِبَ عَلِيٌّ شَيْئًا. وَلَوْ كَانَ هَذَا يُوجِبُ الْعِلْمَ لَشَرِكَهُ فِي ذَلِكَ كُلُّ مَنْ حَضَرَ، وَلَمْ يَرْوِ هَذَا أَحَدٌ مِنْ أَهْلِ الْعِلْمِ.

وَكَذَلِكَ مَا يُذْكَرُ أَنَّهُ كَانَ عِنْدَهُ عِلْمٌ بَاطِنٌ امْتَازَ بِهِ عَنْ أَبِي بَكْرٍ وَعُمَرَ وَغَيْرِهِمَا، فَهَذَا مِنْ مَقَالَاتِ الْمَلَاحِدَةِ الْبَاطِنِيَّةِ وَنَحْوِهِمْ الَّذِينَ هُمْ أَكْفَرُ مِنْهُمْ.

In fact, they (the heretical esoteresists ) embody disbelief that is not even embodied by the Jews and Christians, such as the belief in the divinity and prophethood of ʿAlī, his superiority to the Prophet ﷺ in knowledge, the belief that ʿAlī inwardly was the Prophet's teacher, and similar beliefs that are only espoused by those extreme in disbelief and heresy.(1)

Allah (glorified and exalted He be) knows best.

(1) These notions may seem preposterous today; however, there has been a wide array of extremist Shi'ite sects and heretics across history that maintained similar heretical beliefs. Furthermore, the notion of *tafwīḍ*, which is the belief that ʿAlī ibn Abī Ṭālib is the secondary creator of the entire universe, is gaining traction in some Twelver circles today, even though it is also regarded as *ghulū* in many other Twelver circles. It should not come as a surprise to us if we later observe such preposterous beliefs becoming normalized in a subset of future Shi'ite circles.

بَلْ فِيهِمْ مِنَ الْكُفْرِ مَا لَيْسَ فِي الْيَهُودِ وَالنَّصَارَى، كَالَّذِينَ يَعْتَقِدُونَ إِلَهِيَّتَهُ وَنُبُوَّتَهُ وَأَنَّهُ كَانَ أَعْلَمَ مِنَ النَّبِيِّ ﷺ، وَأَنَّهُ كَانَ مُعَلِّمًا لِلنَّبِيِّ ﷺ فِي الْبَاطِنِ؛ وَنَحْوِ هَذِهِ الْمَقَالَاتِ الَّتِي إِنَّمَا يَقُولُهَا الْغُلَاةُ فِي الْكُفْرِ وَالْإِلْحَادِ.

وَاللَّهُ سُبْحَانَهُ وَتَعَالَى أَعْلَمُ.

# Fatwā #4
# On the Repentance of a Rāfiḍī

## The Question

Ibn Taymiyya (Allah bestow mercy upon him) was asked about two men who disputed with each other on one who curses Abū Bakr. One of them said, "Allah shall forgive him," and the other said, "Allah shall not forgive him."(1)

## The Answer

He responded:

The correct position upheld by the *Imāms* of the Muslims is that anyone who repents to Allah shall be forgiven by Allah. As Allah said, "Say, 'O My servants who have transgressed against themselves: do not despair of Allah's mercy, for Allah forgives all sins. He is indeed the Forgiver, the Clement'. [Quran 39:53]" Allah mentioned in this verse that He pardons all sins of the repentant. For that reason, He spoke in unconditional and general terms.

In another verse, He said, "God does not forgive association with Him, but He forgives anything less than that to whomever He wills. [Quran 4:38]" This verse refers to the non-repentant. For that reason, He spoke in restrictive and exclusive terms.

---

(1) Majmūʿ al-Fatāwā (4/528)

# الفتوى الرابعة

## الجواب على من قال: لا يتوب الله على سابِّ أبي بكر رضي الله عنه

### السؤال

سُئِلَ - رحمه الله - عَنْ رَجُلَيْنِ تَنَازَعَا فِي سَابِّ أَبِي بَكْرٍ. أَحَدُهُمَا يَقُولُ: يَتُوبُ اللَّهُ عَلَيْهِ؛ وَقَالَ الْآخَرُ: لَا يَتُوبُ اللَّهُ عَلَيْهِ.

### الجواب

فَأَجَابَ:

الصَّوَابُ الَّذِي عَلَيْهِ أَئِمَّةُ الْمُسْلِمِينَ أَنَّ كُلَّ مَنْ تَابَ تَابَ اللَّهُ عَلَيْهِ، كَمَا قَالَ اللَّهُ تَعَالَى: {قُلْ يَا عِبَادِيَ الَّذِينَ أَسْرَفُوا عَلَى أَنْفُسِهِمْ لَا تَقْنَطُوا مِنْ رَحْمَةِ اللَّهِ إِنَّ اللَّهَ يَغْفِرُ الذُّنُوبَ جَمِيعًا إِنَّهُ هُوَ الْغَفُورُ الرَّحِيمُ}. فَقَدْ ذَكَرَ فِي هَذِهِ الْآيَةِ أَنَّهُ يَغْفِرُ لِلتَّائِبِ الذُّنُوبَ جَمِيعًا، وَلِهَذَا أَطْلَقَ وَعَمَّمَ.

وَقَالَ فِي الْآيَةِ الْأُخْرَى: {إِنَّ اللَّهَ لَا يَغْفِرُ أَنْ يُشْرَكَ بِهِ وَيَغْفِرُ مَا دُونَ ذَلِكَ لِمَنْ يَشَاءُ}، فَهَذَا فِي غَيْرِ التَّائِبِ، وَلِهَذَا قَيَّدَ وَخَصَّصَ.

Cursing the *Ṣaḥāba* is not a worse sin than cursing the prophets or cursing Allah (exalted He be). Per consensus of the Muslims, if the Jews and Christians who curse our Prophet ﷺ in private among themselves repent and embrace Islam, it is accepted from them. As for the ḥadīth that is reported, which says, "Cursing my companions is an unforgivable sin," it is a lie about the Messenger of Allah.(1)

Per consensus of the Muslims, even polytheism (*shirk*), which Allah does not forgive, is forgiven for whomever repents.

Regarding what is claimed that [cursing] involves the right of a person [who is wronged], it is to be addressed in two ways.

One of them is that Allah has mandated the repentence of both the thief and the one who insults others with demeaning nicknames. As Allah said, "As for the thief, whether male or female, cut their hands as a penalty for what they have reaped—a deterrent from Allah. Allah is Mighty and Wise. But whoever repents after his crime and reforms, Allah will accept his repentance. Allah is Forgiving and Merciful. [Quran 5:39]" Allah also said, "Nor shall you insult one another with names. Evil is the return to wickedness after having attained faith. Whoever does not repent—these are the wrongdoers. [Quran 49:11]" Part of such a person's repentance process is that he compensate the harmed person with goodness in proportion to his transgression against him.

---

(1) No ḥadīth with this wording is reported in the renowned ḥadīth collections. I was later informed by an article written by Sheikh Muḥammad Ziyād Al-Tukla that the ḥadīth scholar, Ibn al-Ṣalāḥ, described this tradition, saying, "It is from the ḥadīths of the laity that have no known basis." See Fatāwā wa-Masā'il Ibn al-Ṣalāḥ (1/188-191). Sheikh Al-Tukla's article can be accessed through the following link:

https://www.alukah.net/sharia/0/51137/%D8%AD%D8%AF%D9%8A%D8%AB-%D8%B3%D8%A8-%D8%A3%D8%B5%D8%AD%D8%A7%D8%A8%D9%8A-%D8%B0%D9%86%D8%A8-%D9%84%D8%A7-%D9%8A%D8%BA%D9%81%D8%B1/

وَلَيْسَ سَبُّ بَعْضِ الصَّحَابَةِ بِأَعْظَمَ مِنْ سَبِّ الْأَنْبِيَاءِ أَوْ سَبِّ اللَّهِ تَعَالَى. والْيَهُودُ وَالنَّصَارَى الَّذِينَ يَسُبُّونَ نَبِيَّنَا سِرًّا بَيْنَهُمْ إِذَا تَابُوا وَأَسْلَمُوا قُبِلَ ذَلِكَ مِنْهُمْ بِاتِّفَاقِ الْمُسْلِمِينَ. وَالْحَدِيثُ الَّذِي يُرْوَى: {سَبُّ صَحَابَتِي ذَنْبٌ لَا يُغْفَرُ} كَذِبٌ عَلَى رَسُولِ ﷺ.

وَالشِّرْكُ الَّذِي لَا يَغْفِرُهُ اللَّهُ يَغْفِرُهُ لِمَنْ تَابَ بِاتِّفَاقِ الْمُسْلِمِينَ.

وَمَا يُقَالُ إِنَّ فِي ذَلِكَ حَقًّا لِآدَمِيٍّ يُجَابُ عَنْهُ مِنْ وَجْهَيْنِ:

أَحَدُهُمَا: أَنَّ اللَّهَ قَدْ أَمَرَ بِتَوْبَةِ السَّارِقِ والْمُلَقِّبِ وَنَحْوِهِمَا مِنَ الذُّنُوبِ الَّتِي تَعَلَّقَ بِهَا حُقُوقُ الْعِبَادِ، كَقَوْلِهِ: {وَالسَّارِقُ وَالسَّارِقَةُ فَاقْطَعُوا أَيْدِيَهُمَا جَزَاءً بِمَا كَسَبَا نَكَالًا مِنَ اللَّهِ وَاللَّهُ عَزِيزٌ حَكِيمٌ . فَمَنْ تَابَ مِنْ بَعْدِ ظُلْمِهِ وَأَصْلَحَ فَإِنَّ اللَّهَ يَتُوبُ عَلَيْهِ إِنَّ اللَّهَ غَفُورٌ رَحِيمٌ}. وَقَالَ: {وَلَا تَنَابَزُوا بِالْأَلْقَابِ بِئْسَ الِاسْمُ الْفُسُوقُ بَعْدَ الْإِيمَانِ وَمَنْ لَمْ يَتُبْ فَأُولَئِكَ هُمُ الظَّالِمُونَ}. وَمِنْ تَوْبَةِ مِثْلِ هَذَا أَنْ يُعَوِّضَ الْمَظْلُومُ مِنَ الْإِحْسَانِ إِلَيْهِ بِقَدْرِ إِسَاءَتِهِ إِلَيْهِ.

The second issue is that those [who curse the *Ṣaḥāba*] do so via *ta'wīl*.[1] Thus, if the Rāfiḍī repents from that, believes in the virtuousness of the *Ṣaḥāba*, loves them, and supplicates for them, then Allah has replaced his sin with a good deed, as is the case with other sinners.

(1) This term refers to erroneous interpretation of scripture and religious ordinances that results in flawed conclusions which are mistakenly believed to be sanctioned within Islam.

الْوَجْهُ الثَّانِي: أَنَّ هَؤُلَاءِ مُتَأَوِّلُونَ، فَإِذَا تَابَ الرافضي مِنْ ذَلِكَ وَاعْتَقَدَ فَضْلَ الصَّحَابَةِ وَأَحَبَّهُمْ وَدَعَا لَهُمْ فَقَدْ بَدَّلَ اللَّهُ السَّيِّئَةَ بِالْحَسَنَةِ كَغَيْرِهِ مِنَ الْمُذْنِبِينَ.

# Fatwā #5
# On the Claim that Rāfiḍīs are Worse than Jews and Christians

## The Question

Ibn Taymiyya (Allah bestow mercy upon him) was asked about a man who deems the Jews and Christians better than the Rāfiḍa.(1)

## The Answer

He responded:

All praise be to Allah. Every individual who believes in what was brought by Muḥammad ﷺ is better than all those who disbelieved in him. This holds true even if the believer embodies a type of innovation (*bidʿa*), be it the *bidʿa* of the Kharijites, Shia, Murjiʾa, Qadariyya or others.

The Jews and Christians are disbelievers who embody definitive disbelief that is known by necessity per the religion of Islam. As for the innovator (*mubtadiʿ*), if he believes he is aligning with the Prophet ﷺ and not opposing him, then he has not disbelieved in him. Even if he fall into disbelief [due to his innovation], his disbelief is incomparable to the disbelief of those who impugned the Messenger of Allah ﷺ.(2)

---

(1) Majmūʿ al-Fatāwā (35/201)

(2) Imām al-Ḍahabī similarly remarked in *Siyar Aʿlām al-Nubalāʾ*, saying, "Anyone who is declared a disbeliever due to an innovation (*bidʿa*), even if the innovation is severe, is not comparable to the original disbeliever, nor the Jew, nor the Zoroastrian. Allah has refused to equate one who believed in Allah, His Messenger and the Final Day, fasted prayed, and gave *zakat*

# الفتوى الخامسة

## في الجواب على مَن فضّل أهلَ الكتاب على الرّافضة

### السؤال

وَسُئِلَ – رَحِمَهُ اللَّهُ تَعَالَى – عَنْ رَجُلٍ يُفَضِّلُ الْيَهُودَ وَالنَّصَارَى عَلَى الرَّافِضَةِ.

### الجواب

فَأَجَابَ:

الْحَمْدُ لِلَّهِ. كُلُّ مَنْ كَانَ مُؤْمِنًا بِمَا جَاءَ بِهِ مُحَمَّدٌ ﷺ فَهُوَ خَيْرٌ مِنْ كُلِّ مَنْ كَفَرَ بِهِ، وَإِنْ كَانَ فِي الْمُؤْمِنِ بِذَلِكَ نَوْعٌ مِنَ الْبِدْعَةِ – سَوَاءٌ كَانَتْ بِدْعَةَ الْخَوَارِجِ وَالشِّيعَةِ وَالْمُرْجِئَةِ وَالْقَدَرِيَّةِ أَوْ غَيْرِهِمْ.

فَإِنَّ الْيَهُودَ وَالنَّصَارَى كُفَّارٌ كُفْرًا مَعْلُومًا بِالِاضْطِرَارِ مِنْ دِينِ الْإِسْلَامِ. وَالْمُبْتَدِعُ إِذَا كَانَ يَحْسَبُ أَنَّهُ مُوَافِقٌ لِلرَّسُولِ ﷺ لَا مُخَالِفٌ لَهُ لَمْ يَكُنْ كَافِرًا بِهِ. وَلَوْ قُدِّرَ أَنَّهُ يَكْفُرُ فَلَيْسَ كُفْرُهُ مِثْلَ كُفْرِ مَنْ كَذَّبَ الرَّسُولَ ﷺ.

---

with one who resisted the Messenger, worshipped the idol, rejected the religious ordinances (*sharāʾiʿ*), and disbelieved. We disassociate before Allah from the innovations (*bidaʿ*) and their people.” See Siyar Aʿlām al-Nubalāʾ of al-Ḍahābī (10/202).

# Bibliography

Al-ʾĀjurrī, Muḥammad ibn al-Ḥusayn, *Kitāb al-Sharīʿa*, ʿAbdullāh Al-Dumayjī, ed., 1st ed., (Riyadh, 1418/1997).

Al-Aṣbahānī, Abū Nuʿaym Aḥmed ibn ʿAbdillāh, *Ḥilyat al-Awliyāʾ wa-Ṭabaqāt al-Aṣfiyāʾ*, Beirut, 1996/1416.

Al-Baghdādī, al-Khaṭīb Aḥmed ibn ʿAlī ibn Thābit, *al-Faṣl li-l-Waṣl al-Mudraj Fī al-Naql*, Muḥammad Al-Zahrānī, ed., 1st ed., (Riyadh, 1418/1997).

——. *al-Kifāya Fī Maʿrifat Uṣūl ʿIlm al-Riwāya*, Māhir Al-Faḥl, ed., 3rd ed., (Dammam, 1441).

Al-Buhūtī, Manṣūr ibn Yūnus, *al-Rawḍ al-Murbiʿ Sharḥ Zād al-Mustaqniʿ*, Turkī ibn Saʿūd Al-Dhiyābī, ed., 1st ed., (Dammam, 1440).

Al-Bukhārī, Muḥammad ibn Ismāʿīl, *Ṣaḥīḥ al-Bukhārī*, Muḥammad Zuhayr Al-Nāṣir, ed., 1st ed., (Beirut, 1423).

Al-Ḍabbī, Muḥammad ibn Khalaf, *Akhbār al-Quḍāt*, ʿAbdulʿAzīz Al-Marāghī, ed., 1st ed., (Cairo, 1366/1947).

Al-Ḏahabī, Muḥammad ibn Aḥmed ibn ʿUthmān, *Siyar Aʿlām al-Nubalāʾ*, Shuʿayb Al-Arnāʾūṭ et al., eds., 1st ed., (Beirut, 1402/1982).

——. *Tārīkh al-Islām*, Bashār ʿAwwād Maʿrūf, ed., 1st ed., (Beirut, 2003).

Al-Ḥalabī, ʿAlī ibn Ibrāhīm, *al-Sīra al-Ḥalabiyya*, 2nd ed., (Beirut, 1427).

Ibn ʿAbdilHādī, Muḥammad ibn Aḥmed, *Majmūʿ Rasāʾil al-Ḥāfiẓ Ibn ʿAbdilHādī*, Ḥusayn bin ʿUkāsha, ed., 1st ed., (Cairo, 1427/2006).

Ibn Abī Ḥātim, ʿAbdurraḥmān ibn Muḥammad ibn Idrīs, *Kitāb ʿIlal al-Ḥadīth*, Saʿd Al-Ḥumayyid et al., eds., 1st ed., (Riyadh, 1427/2006).

Ibn Abī Khaythama, Aḥmed ibn Zuhayr, *al-Tārīkh al-Kabīr – al-Sifr al-Thālith*, Ṣalāḥ Halal, ed., 1st ed., (Cairo, 1423/2004).

Ibn Abī Shayba, Abū Bakr ʿAbdullāh, *al-Muṣannaf*, Muḥammad ʿAwwāma, ed., 1st ed., (Beirut, 1427/2006).

Ibn ʿAdī, ʿAbdullāh, *al-Kāmil Fī Ḍuʿafāʾ al-Rijāl*, Muḥammad Al-Khin, ed., 1st ed., (Damascus, 1433/2012).

Ibn ʿAsākir, ʿAlī ibn al-Ḥasan, *Tārīkh Dimashq*, ʿAmr Al-ʿAmrawī, ed., 1st ed., (Beirut, 1415-1417/1995-1996).

Ibn al-Farrāʾ, al-Qāḍī Abū Yaʿlā Muḥammad ibn al-Ḥusayn, *al-ʿUdda Fī Uṣūl al-Fiqh*, Aḥmed Al-Mubarakī, ed., 3rd ed., (Riyadh, 1414/1993).

Ibn Ḥajar, Aḥmed ibn ʿAlī, *Fatḥ al-Bārī Sharḥ Ṣaḥīḥ al-Bukhārī*, Muḥib Al-Khaṭīb, ed., Beirut, 1379.

Ibn Ḥanbal, Aḥmed ibn Muḥammad, *Musnad al-Imām Aḥmed Ibn Ḥanbal*, Shuʿayb Al-Arnāʾūṭ et al., eds., 1st ed., (Beirut, 1421/2001).

Ibn Ḥazm, ʿAlī ibn Aḥmed, *al-Faṣl Fī al-Milal wa-l-ʾAhwāʾ wa-l-Niḥal*, Muḥammad Naṣr and ʿAbdurraḥmān ʿUmayra, eds., 2nd ed., (Beirut, 1416/1996).

Ibn Ḥibbān, Muḥammad, *Ṣaḥīḥ Ibn Ḥibbān*, Muḥammad ʿAlī Sonmez and Khāliṣ Aydemīr, eds., 1st ed., (Beirut, 1433/2012).

Ibn Hishām, ʿAbdulMalik ibn Hishām, *al-Sīra al-Nabawayiyya*, Muṣtafā al-Saqqā et al, eds., 8th ed., (Beirut, 1433/2012).

Ibn al-Jawzī, ʿAbdurraḥmān ibn ʿAlī, *Kitāb al-Mawḍūʿāt*, ʿAbdurraḥmān Muḥammad ʿUthmān, ed., 1st ed., (Medina, 1386/1966).

Ibn Kathīr, Ismāʿīl ibn ʿUmar, *al-Bidāya wa-l-Nihāya*, ʿAbdullāh al-Turkī, ed., 1st ed., (Cairo, 1418/1997).

Ibn Khayyāṭ, Khalīfa, *Tārīkh Khalīfa ibn Khayyāṭ*, Akram Ḍiyāʾ Al-ʿUmarī, ed., 2nd ed., (Riyadh, 1405-1985).

Ibn Khuzayma, Muḥammad ibn Isḥāq, *Ṣaḥīḥ Ibn Khuzayma*, Muḥammad Muṣṭafā al-Aʿẓamī, ed., 3rd ed., (Riyadh, 1420/2009).

Ibn Māja, Muḥammad ibn Yazīd, *Sunan Ibn Māja*, Shuʿayb al-Arnāʾūṭ et al, eds., 1st ed., (Damascus, 1430/2009).

Ibn Manṣūr, Saʿīd, *Sunan Saʿīd ibn Manṣūr*, Ḥabīb Al-Raḥmān Al-ʾAʿẓamī, ed., 1st ed., (Bombay, 1403/1982).

Ibn al-Qayyim, Muḥammad ibn Abī Bakr, *Iʿlām al-Muwaqqiʿīn ʿAn Rabb al-ʿĀlamīn*, Mashhūr bin Ḥasan Āl Salmām, ed., 1st ed., (Dammam, 1423).

Ibn Qudāma, ʿAbdullāh ibn Aḥmed, *al-Muntakhab Min ʿIlal al-Khallāl*, Ṭāriq bin ʿAwaḍAllāh, ed., 1st ed., (Riyadh, 1419, 1998).

Ibn Saʿd, Muḥammad, *al-Ṭabaqāt al-Kabīr*, ʿAlī Muḥammad ʿUmar, ed., 1st ed., (Cairo, 1421/2001).

Ibn al-Ṣalāḥ, ʿUthmān ibn Ṣalāḥ al-Dīn, *Fatāwā wa-Masāʾil Ibn al-Ṣalāḥ Fī al-Tafsīr wa-l-Ḥadīth wa-l-Uṣūl wa-l-Fiqh*, ʿAbdulMuʿṭī Qalʿajī, ed., 1st ed., (Beirut, 1406/1986).

Ibn Sallām, al-Qāsim, *Kitāb al-ʾAmwāl*, Sayyid bin Rajab, ed., 1st ed., (El Mansoura, 1428/2007)

Ibn Shabba, ʿUmar ibn Shabba, *Tārīkh al-Madīna al-Munawwara*, Fahīm Shaltūt, ed., Jeddah, 1399.

Ibn Taymiyya, Aḥmed ibn ʿAbdilḤalīm, *Majmūʿ al-Fatāwā*, ʿAbdurraḥmān ibn Muḥammad ibn Qāsim, ed., Medina, 1425/2004.

——. *Minhāj al-Sunnah al-Nabawiyya Fī Naqḍ Kalām al-Shīʿa wa-l-Qadariyya*, Muḥammad Sālim, ed., 1st ed., (Riyadh, 1406/1986).

Al-Jāḥiẓ, ʿAmr ibn Baḥr, *al-ʿUthmāniyya*, ʿAbdulSalām Hārūn, ed., 1st ed., (Beirut, 1411/1991).

Al-Jawharī, ʿAbdurraḥmān ibn ʿAbdillāh, *Musnad al-Muwaṭṭaʾ*, Luṭfī Al-Ṣaghīr and Ṭāḥa Būsrīʿ, eds., 1st ed., (Beirut, 1997).

Al-Juwaynī, ʿAbdulMalik ibn ʿAbdillāh, *Nihāyat al-Maṭlab Fī Dirāyat al-Maḏhab*, ʿAbdulʿAẓīm Maḥmūd al-Dīb, ed., 1st ed., (Jeddah, 1428/2007).

Al-Khallāl, Abū Bakr Aḥmed ibn Muḥammad, *Kitāb al-Sunnah*, ʿAṭiyya Al-Zahrānī, ed., 1st ed., (Riyadh, 1410/1989).

Al-Kulaynī, Muḥammad ibn Yaʿqūb, *Kitāb al-Kāfī*, 1st ed., (Beirut, 1428/2007).

Al-Nawawī, Yaḥyā ibn Sharaf, *al-Majmūʿ Sharḥ al-Muhaḏḏab*, Cairo, n.d.

Al-Naysābūrī, al-Ḥākim Muḥammad ibn ʿAbdillāh, *al-Mustadrak ʿalā al-Ṣaḥīḥayn*, 1st ed., (Cairo,1435/2014).

Al-Naysābūrī, Muslim b. al-Ḥajjāj, *Ṣaḥīḥ Muslim*, Muḥammad Fuʾād ʿAbdilBāqī, ed., 1st ed., (Cairo, 1412/1991).

Al-Mūsawī, al-Sharīf al-Murtaḍā ʿAlī ibn al-Ḥusayn, *al-Intiṣār*, Najaf, 1971.

Qāḍī al-Māristān, Muḥammad ibn ʿAbdilBāqī, *al-Mashyakha al-Kubrā*, Ḥātem Al-ʿAwnī, ed., 1st ed., (Mecca, 1422).

Al-Ṣaffār, Muḥammad ibn al-Ḥasan, *Baṣāʾir al-Darajār*, 1st ed., (Beirut, 1431/2010).

Al-Ṣanʿānī, ʿAbdurrazzāq b. Hammām, *al-Muṣannaf*, Ḥabīb Al-Raḥmān Al-ʿAẓmī, ed., 2nd ed., (Beirut, 1403).

Al-Sijistānī, Abū Dāwūd Sulaymān ibn al-Ashʿath, *Masāʾil al-Imām Aḥmed – Riwāyat Abī Dāwūd al-Sijistānī*, Ṭāriq ʿAwaḍallāh, ed., 1st ed., (Egypt, 1420/1999).

Al-Suhaylī, ʿAbdurraḥmān ibn ʿAbdillāh, *al-Rawḍ al-ʾUnuf Fī Sharḥ al-Sīra al-Nabawiyya li-Ibn Hishām*, ʿAbdurraḥmān Al-Wakīl, ed., 1st ed., (Cairo, 1387/1967).

Al-Tirmiḏī, Muḥammad ibn ʿĪsā, *al-Jāmiʿ al-Kabīr*, Bashār ʿAwwād Maʿrūf, ed., 1st ed., (Beirut, 1996).

Al-ʿUqaylī, Muḥammad ibn ʿAmr, *Kitāb al-Ḍuʿafāʾ al-Kabīr*, ʿAbdulMuʿṭī Qalʿajī, ed., 1st ed., (Beirut, n.d.).

Al-Wāqidī, Muḥammad ibn ʿUmar, *Kitāb al-Maghāzī*, Marseden Jones, ed., 1st ed., (Beirut, 1427/2006).

Al-Yaḥṣubī, al-Qāḍī ʿIyāḍ, *al-Shifā Bi-Taʿrīf Ḥuqūq al-Muṣṭafā*, 1st ed., ʿAbduh Kūshak, ed., (Dubai, 1434/2013).

www.ingramcontent.com/pod-product-compliance
Lightning Source LLC
LaVergne TN
LVHW021134080426
835509LV00010B/1353
*9798218293451*